Aspirational Revolution

This book is dedicated to my wife, Ashley, for she is my own purpose. Though it is your aspiration for me that I do something important for the sake of helping the world, it is only for you that I strive to do something worthy of your respect, your admiration, and your love. You said you wanted a zombie book dedicated to you, but it seemed that it could not be more appropriate than to dedicate to you a book about the importance of having purpose in life. For it is you that inspires me to pursue something meaningful, who gives me the courage to do so, and who makes that pursuit worth the effort. You have made the world a better place in your own way, and have pushed me to help make it better in mine. You have wished for a better world, and it is for you that I will work toward creating it.

Puff!

PREFACE

Academic books such as this one tend to be very expensive. In my past experiences publishing with Palgrave Macmillan, each of my books were priced retail at over $100 each. That means if you are reading this, you are extremely passionate or serious about the contents within. Either you have accessed this book online through your resources at work, or you have deemed that it was worth the high price to buy this book. In any case, odds are that you work in the field. Although the editors at Palgrave assure me that this pricing makes sense for the market, the contents of this book in particular have a relevance for people outside of academia—people who either cannot or will not pay such a high price premium on a book that is not directly related to their professional work.

The nature of this book is relevant right now—today. There is a lot of talk about universal basic income, economic reforms, work automation, and so forth. Even if people do not work in economics, they have a lot of questions about these things and want to know more. As such, if you have read this book, I ask that you share it with others. Think of someone who would not otherwise buy this book due to cost constraints or a lack of awareness that it even exists, and either let them borrow it or simply give it away, if you are so inclined. No matter how you go about it, the point is simply that the vast majority of the population will not have access to the information contained within this book—information that is entirely unique an unavailable anywhere else in the world—and it is my hope that you will help to change that. The publisher would approve, since sharing this book with someone outside their target market will not cut into their sales, and it will give the book greater public exposure outside of their traditional distribution channels. I, as the author, would just be happy to know that people are reading the book. They are not paying me enough to be concerned with trying to sell books for the sake of money, so my incentive is purely to make this information as widely available as possible. Just do not make copies of the book or copy the contents online, because that would be a violation of copyright law which could get you in legal trouble. Lawyers are probably the only people more dismal than economists, so let us keep them out of it.

There is a very legitimate point to this request: As you will come to find, it is one of the core principles of economic growth and development that knowledge be shared, ideally with as many people as possible. It is this knowledge sharing which creates innovation. As a result, by sharing this book, you are taking a tangible action to participate in the very methods of advancing humanity which is described in the book you are sharing. As a reader of this book, if you are inspired to take an action as small as simply allowing someone else borrow the book, then that person might become inspired to pursue their own passions, making a real difference not only in their lives, but contributing to our future economic well-being. In other words, by providing this book to those who would otherwise not find it accessible due to matters of distribution or price, the book itself becomes a part of the mechanisms described within it. Each time this book is shared with another person, there is the chance that the person will pursue their own sense of purpose and create a positive change by doing so.

My request to share this book is about more than that, though. Scientists, mathematicians, economists, and other specialized professionals seem to have a difficult time communicating with the public. For many, they have trouble explaining their work in ways that make sense to people who do not work in the field. For others, there is a difficulty in communicating their work in a way that is interesting and/or relevant to the people they are trying to reach (in other words, many people working in technical fields tend to be boring when they are talking about their work). Science magazines and news seem to hurt as much as they help, in that research is often misrepresented or misinterpreted either because even the reporter does not understand the nature of the topic, or because they, themselves, are having difficulty making the topic interesting to readers. "Sensationalism" is a real problem (Kendall and Smoliga 2017).

Throughout history there have been people who are very successful at educating the public about how the world works. Michael Faraday, Carl

Sagan, Bill Nye, Neil DeGrasse Tyson... all these people have carried-on a tradition of making modern research topics accessible to the public. While I do not count myself among them, it is important that the effort at least be made to properly inform the public. It is vital to the progress of a functional society that people understand how the world around them works, and it is crucial for a healthy democracy that the public be well-informed about the topics upon which they are voting. Economics is not always an easy subject, nor is it always an interesting one (except this book because this book is amazing), but it permeates every aspect of our lives, and since we have put so much of our economic policy into the hands of politicians it is necessary that people understand at least the relevant aspects of applied economics because the public will be the ones voting for who makes economic decisions. No, I am not talking about the stuff from your Econ 101 and Econ 102 courses, either. Intro economics uses a lot of tools and concepts to help you understand the fundamentals, but those tools and concepts are ultimately so filled with assumptions as to be completely useless in a functional setting. So, we are going to be talking about more advanced economic matters—things which actually work. That is why this book is written as simply as possible, including short explanations of some basic concepts that the target buyer probably already knows; and this is why I have included narratives and examples in the style of a motivational book, hopefully helping to make the book a bit more interesting. By doing this, and by encouraging you to share this book with those who would otherwise not read it, I am making my very small contribution to helping to improve the public's knowledge of economics, of society, and of behavioral science.

Thanks.

Beulah, MI, USA   Michael Taillard

Bibliography
Smoliga, J. M., & Kendall, C. J. (2017). Inaccuracies: Axe science hype from social media. *Nature, 542*(7639), 31–31. doi:10.1038/542031c.

ACKNOWLEDGEMENTS

I would like to offer special thanks to everyone who shared their personal stories. It is not an easy thing to make any part of your personal life available for public viewing, much less those events which have caused us to overcome challenges, but by sharing your experiences you have helped to illustrate some very important principles throughout this book. You have provided an invaluable service to me and to the readers of this book, and contributed greatly to any progress that might develop as a result of this book being published. That you did it for free is especially appreciative. Thank you!

CONTENTS

LIST OF FIGURES

List of Tables

Introduction

That which you are about to read spans that chasm between rigorous scientific exploration and predictive dreamscape. The contents of this book are new ideas which have been left completely unexplored until this time, and yet they are also purely a natural extension of those things which have already been proven. This is a look at a future which could be—one option among many based on the ways society might respond to the economic challenges set before us, as we attempt to overcome them through the application of well-proven fundamentals of economics as they are applied to modern raw data. The pages contained within the book will present to you an argument that these new ideas—this single proposal for a new economic paradigm—are the optimal path forward by blending econometric facts, narratives of actual people and circumstances, and just a bit of inspired creativity—what Einstein might call a "thought experiment".

Simply put, this book demonstrates a fiscal system which is intended to facilitate mass-innovation by tapping into the whole of unutilized or underutilized knowledge and effort among the total national or global population. There are limits to the physical efforts of man and machine, and within the context of the current challenges we endeavor to overcome, these limits and the restrictions they place on humanity's ability to advance itself are proving to put quite a definitive completion upon the attempt. It is a certainty, however, that by utilizing an optimal structure through which the maximum number of people contribute to the pool of knowledge and innovation, facilitating the ever-growing potential of those who compose the entirety of the labor force, that the very limits currently placed upon

© The Author(s) 2017
M. Taillard, *Aspirational Revolution*,
DOI 10.1007/978-3-319-61771-8_1

human advancement are lifted. Perhaps this will allow us to expand beyond what we today perceive as the global finale, or perhaps this will merely allow to truly know the limits of what is possible within that time; but whether by invention, market competition, scientific discovery, artistic expression, or any other method by which a person might endeavor to extend the boundaries of human capability, it is a necessity of our continued progress that we should do all that is possible to assist in their effort.

Around the world there are people with great ideas, exceptional skill, and unique inspiration who are excluded from the pool of available knowledge. Our current economic system simply does not allow for them to fully contribute their value to society, and as a result humanity is stunted, never advancing at the rate of which it is capable. The nation which adopts a system such that opportunities are provided to stimulate the inspiration of the general population would experience an unprecedented acceleration in both growth and development, becoming an engine of progress driven by its ability to self-perpetuate its own expansion of knowledge. It is only by tapping into sources of knowledge, creativity, and competition that have been left completely unutilized by the current system of exclusionary markets that this can be accomplished. Although other recent proposals intended to accomplish this have been explored more thoroughly, it is within this book that a new, and demonstrably superior, possibility is proposed.

This is a proposal that will undoubtedly be considered controversial. It is not controversial in the sense that it is offensive, but rather in that it delves into conclusions about the future of economics which the world has never seen before. We are now experiencing within the overall economic paradigm changes which are, by necessity, occurring very quickly. Since these changes are quite new there is yet little agreement on their exact nature, and the actual logistics of optimally adapting to them becomes a matter of informed speculation supported as best as possible by evidence. As such, there are guaranteed to be those who will debate the methods proposed in this book, and I should hope they do, since it is through such discourse that solutions are devised and books are sold.

Yet, despite the debate which this book will inevitably spur, it is agreed upon nearly universally that we have entered a period of fundamental change—that our ability to continue sustaining economic growth and improving quality of life is now reaching its upper limits under the current structure, and that we are seeing hints of a new paradigm just as revolutionary as the inceptions of agriculture or industrialization. In order for us to make the next big leap in human progress, though, we must first prepare to implement an economic structure which is capable of facilitating this change. The discussions on this matter have, thus far, been insufficient, as they are built entirely within the current paradigm which we must now transcend. All solutions born of the current dynamic is inevitably doomed to fail.

Though being wholly new, and such a dramatic shift from the current paradigm, the conclusions upon which the proposed structure in this book is based are inescapable, being mere logical extensions of a unique set of well-established facts and the most basic of economic principles. There are no unproven assertions, no questionable experiments, no unorthodox interpretations, and no vague statistical distinctions used within this book. There is no specialized prerequisite knowledge necessary, or assumptions which one must begrudgingly accept for the sake of argument, to come to the same conclusions on your own. Simply put, the problem addressed in this book and the matters from which the solution is derived are all well-known, basic economics. Even the solution, in its own way, is already known, though perhaps left unrecognized; or at the very least left as a vague theoretical construct without an established method of application. In any case, though the content of this missing piece of the puzzle may surprise, upon reflection it becomes clear that it could be nothing else.

This book is written with a duality. Much of it is written as simply as possible partially to demonstrate how the proposed economic paradigm is merely a natural extension of established facts and principles left unexplored. These portions are also written in a manner that does not require a prerequisite understanding of economics in the hope that any person can look to this book and find the inspiration they need to truly apply their underutilized potential. After all, though being distributed by an academic publisher, the book truly is about those unappreciated individuals who are achieving less than they could be, and the amount of importance they will have in the not-so-distant future under a new economic paradigm. Then, particularly in the second half of the book, there are elements which delve heavily into more complex modeling and functions. This is necessary to demonstrate the solid foundations upon which the proposed paradigm are built, and to explain the context of its validation within the framework of economic theory. It is not that this content is any more difficult to read, but rather that it is more specialized, and will be in many ways unfamiliar to the casual reader. These portions, too, will be written as simply as possible, and will still not require any prerequisite knowledge, but may be a bit overwhelming for beginners. Though I would urge you to take your time and familiarize yourself with the occasional handful of jargon, it will not be necessary for you to take from this book its full intent. The end result is a book that anyone can appreciate, with notes of depth catering to the discriminating economist.

Structurally, this book is divided into two portions. If you find the idea of economic growth models to be a bit too dry, then start with Part 1, since this will focus on the individual experiences of people—describing the lives we live within society, and the changes that this society would undergo that would change our lives for the better. If you are looking to get right to the point, then you can even skip the first half and jump right to Part 2. It is in this second half of the book that you will find all the content related to explaining the functional economic mechanisms which are currently driving the world full speed to its own demise, but you will also find the details of the proposed solution which will be used to not only solve the problems we currently face, but which will perpetuate innovation into the future. In other words, Part 2 of this book explains how our economy is broken, and shows how to make it function properly into the indefinite future.

The first portion, *Experience*, explores what it means to strive and survive in the modern era; looking at how the struggles and achievements in life are changing as a result of the current economic revolution from the perspective of the individual. This portion of the book is presented primarily with qualitative, constructivist methods. In other words, the first half of the book is written in a manner that describes reality by telling a story of sorts. It utilizes narrative of the economic implications of the current economic system, explains the impending changes as they could be experienced through select aspects of a typical day, and includes the profiles of real people who represent the underutilized potential to contribute to global developmental progress. In this manner, changes in the very nature of the human experience are described, with the logistics of daily life and the pursuit of purpose emphasized to demonstrate precisely the mechanisms by which productivity and life quality will both improve. That is not to say the first half of this book is devoid of substance—everything is written within the context of explaining the facts and theory of what drives economic growth; but the first half of the book does so in a manner that makes the matter clearly obvious, and viscerally engaging. When things are left purely abstract, it becomes too easy to overlook the obvious, to make false assumptions, or to remove one's self from the reality of daily life for the majority of the world. It also gets tremendously boring. To be blunt, the goal of the first half of the book is to get the point across while holding your attention.

The second portion, *Understand*, describes the theoretical and functional basis for the proposed economic structure. This portion is more typical of what one might expect from a book on economics, and will utilize models, analysis, and the application of established principle. Both applied and abstract views will be taken in demonstrating the events of economic development leading to the modern era, the current problems we face in continuing that development, and why the proposed structure will function as a solution to those problems. This portion is the drier material that details the mechanics of how the new paradigm functions, provides proof within known facts and well-established theories, and utilizes economic modelling as a demonstration of its improvements over competing proposals. This second half of the book then ends on a strong note, with a description of the long-term implications of the proposed structure and what it means for the individual nation(s) which implement it. Looking deep into the effects of applying the proposed paradigm, the final chapter combines a bit of futurism and utopian dreamscape, describing how the paradigm shift will influence the economic dynamics of a nation; of course, remaining grounded to the fundamentals of the field.

As a whole, the second half of the book is built of the macroeconomic foundations that explain the functionality of the structure, and from which the microeconomic experiences and observations of the first half are derived. It is my hope that this will provide both an intellectual and a personal understanding of what the future can be, should we choose to pursue bold new steps which guarantee the revolutionary advancement of human development. If successful, this book will become a self-fulfilling prophecy. For now, though, please relax and enjoy. Maybe you will learn something, maybe you will become inspired to pursue your aspirations, or maybe you will simply appreciate the uniquely sanguine vision for mankind's future as an escape from the daily negativity. In any case, thanks for reading. I hope you enjoy the book.

PART 1

Experience

Economics is a behavioral science, and it is far too often taken for granted that behind all the abstractions and modeling are the decisions and experiences of real people—people who are not living their lives with thoughts of partial derivatives and optimization equations in their heads, but who are simply going about their days in the best way they know. It dehumanizes the economics profession to neglect to tie everything back to the human experience, because ultimately that is the entire point: studying human behavior. That means when we are discussing broad concepts such as growth, we must approach it through an interdisciplinary lens. To talk about economic growth simply as labor and capital is folly, as it ignores such matters as motivation and social engagement and other things which contribute to more familiar economic terms like knowledge spillover (yes, we will elaborate on all this throughout the book, remember that this is an intro chapter, so do not get overwhelmed).

Since it is in the nature of this book that it is introducing brand new ideas, and proposing a brand new paradigm, it seems best to explain it multiple ways. Sure, the second half of the book will get into the hard economics of the matter, but before that—in this first half—we need to establish the context. That means describing what the current paradigm looks like and how it functions. Each chapter in this first half of the book will address one of those issues that shapes peoples' lives and drives them to pursue the paths they have chosen, and even why they did not pursue the path they desired instead. Each chapter will review principles of decision theory within the context of microeconomic environments, providing examples and descriptions of the clockwork behind our collective productive potential. Then to further illustrate the reality of the principles discussed, each chapter will end with a short profile of a real person whose life helps to anecdotally describe what it must be like to experience these matters first-hand, and how they apply to the book. In this way, it will become easier to understand the mechanisms and outcomes inherent in the hard economic proposals discussed in the second half of the book.

Although there is a table of contents in the beginning, and an index in the back, this book is not written or organized in a manner that makes it very simple to use as a reference guide. So, in order to help with that, and make the book a bit more useful in a wider variety of contexts, the introduction to each "part" of this book will provide a list of the chapters included in that part, with a short description of what you will find in each chapter. Some of the basic concepts, principles, terminology, and examples will be provided in these descriptions to help you find your way to what you are looking for without having to search too hard. Hopefully that will prevent you from needing to search through each chapter to find the concepts or constructs you need. That being said, here are the chapters you will find in Part 1: Experience.

CHAPTER 2: A MOST HUMAN STRUGGLE

To be human is to be in constant pursuit of things which often contradict each other. As humans we have evolved a unique survival mechanism: inductive reasoning. It is this trait that has allowed us to thrive as a species by giving us the ability to derive abstract ideas and know how to apply them in innovative new ways without having to directly observe or experience it directly. In the modern era, this unique trait has also created a unique struggle—one wherein people must choose between the mundane acceptance of repetitive production for the sake of earning an income for personal survival and the pursuit to apply our innovative skills which help to assure the survival of our species. Generally speaking, people tend to think they only get to choose one of these options and forego the other. That is not necessarily true, though. This chapter includes an interview with financial consultant Don Mupsey.

CHAPTER 3: THE PURSUIT OF INCOME

It is no longer the pursuit of hunting and farming which allows the majority of people to survive, but the pursuit of income. The pursuit of income has become a critical part of peoples' instinct to survive. By using a combination of Maslow's Hierarchy of Needs and the applied examples of labor markets during the Great Depression, it is shown that this economic paradigm not only causes people to forego even their own personal safety in the pursuit of income, but that this dynamic incentive has, and is, systematically utilized to undermine the negotiating power of workers in the labor market. In the end, it sucks to be poor, and more people would rather risk their lives in the pursuit of steady income, then risk their income in the pursuit of a life. This chapter includes an interview with expatriate English teacher Ty William.

CHAPTER 4: THE PURSUIT OF PASSION

In Chap. 4 we look at motivation—the things which inspire us to create and excel. We turn Maslow on its head and consider whether physiological needs are more important, or just easier to acquire, and consider whether there really is as much risk in pursuing self-actualization where people actually think. Using Herzberg's model and other representations of motivation, we show that survival needs will attract people to forego their other needs, but also contribute to satisficing and freeriding. In the pursuit of passion, quality will shine through and with enough patience, the remainder of peoples' needs will follow. This chapter includes an interview with movie producer and director L. E. Salas.

CHAPTER 5: THE PURSUIT OF FREEDOM

Freedom is critical to an efficient market. The importance of labor mobility alone is a core component of properly matching workers with particular skills with employers who need those skills. So, people must be free to move geographically, they must be free to change companies or start their own, they must be free to learn skills and knowledge or develop entirely new skills and knowledge; they must be free to explore the potential that they find, free of bureaucratic systems and wage slavery.

CHAPTER 6: THE PURSUIT OF EQUALITY

The final chapter of Part 1 is about the growth of income and wealth disparities and the thing which continues to make them grow, which is dubbed National Income Misallocation. The role of labor markets is discussed in this chapter, as the increasing concentration of capital stifles free market competition in product markets but, more importantly, in labor markets. The result is something similar to a monopsony, and labor unions only address the symptoms and not the underlying problem. Professional chef Tony Matta is profiled in this chapter as an example what a real solution will look like.

CHAPTER 2

A Most Human Struggle

It is in the very nature of human evolution that we should struggle in ways no other creature experiences. All living things struggle against the basics of survival; the pursuit of nourishment, avoiding threats, passing on our genes, and so forth. It is not that we struggle in these ways more than any other plant or animal, however. Despite our relatively poor speed and strength, and despite our lack of anything sharp or toxic, and despite being covered in a fragile unarmored flesh that does little to protect or hide us from predators, we actually struggle far less than most creatures against those typical challenges found in the natural world around us. It is the same characteristic of human beings which makes us uniquely able to cope with the environment, however, which is also the exclusive source of a struggle unique to humankind. It is our blessing to be burdened with such a peculiarity, not only because it has allowed us to thrive so successfully, but because it will continue to be the source of human advancement into the entirety of the foreseeable future. We are, of course, talking about the ability to create, but it is more than that.

We have looked to the mind as the source of our advanced state, developing theories about bigger forebrains which allow us to make predictions about cause and effect, but even that is not at all unique to humans. Most animals can use deductive reasoning to learn how to seek rewards and avoid punishments, as was most famously demonstrated by B. F. Skinner in his research on operant conditioning. Many animals learn to use tools, construct solutions, or solve puzzles to achieve their purpose; and it is not just other primates either, but rather a wide variety of mammals and birds,

© The Author(s) 2017
M. Taillard, *Aspirational Revolution*,
DOI 10.1007/978-3-319-61771-8_2

possibly extending even further. In a 2014 study, a team of scientists led by Sarah Jelbert discovered that crows were able to solve puzzles by changing water levels, which puts their deductive reasoning skills roughly at the same level as a 5-year-old human (or anyone who has played the water dungeon in any of several Legend of Zelda games).

That thing which makes humans especially successful in the natural order—the thing of which only people are capable—is inductive reasoning. It is our ability to derive abstract principles from observation and then apply those principles in different ways. This type of abstract thought has allowed us to gain knowledge without direct engagement, to make predictions of things never witnessed, and to find solutions that go well beyond our physical capabilities to problems which were previously beyond our control. Each individual person has their own set of observations which is entirely unique to them, and can therefore offer perspective that is also entirely unique. For those who are inclined to do so, each person who contributes their own inductive capabilities in some novel manner is defining what it means to be human—inherently altering the way in which we engage the world around us, usually for the better. When shared, an abstraction is learned and interpreted by others in unique ways; as each person applies what they already know to it they create new knowledge without ever needing to directly observe. Yet, though humans evolved this novel characteristic that has allowed them to survive and thrive in unparalleled ways, we have failed to fully understand its role in a changing society. The result is a struggle most human: the struggle between survival and purpose.

We are, as a species, perpetual malcontents, instinctually driven to imagine and innovate, and to search for opportunities to benefit from creative pursuits. We have evolved this trait and instinctually apply it, constantly driven by a need to create—constantly developing a better understanding of our environment and society, inherently resulting in the constant discovery of problems which present us with opportunities to create solutions. We have evolved this instinctual need to use inductive reasoning as a way to assure the survival of our species, putting us at the top of the food chain in a manner unique to any other creature, and yet we have organized ourselves in a society which creates ennui. All animals have the instinct to survive as individuals and to protect those familiar to them, but this unique evolutionary instinct to create found within humans so that our species might survive contrasts with those social structures we have created that require people to pursue in banality their instinct to survive as individuals. It is the innately human struggle, then, that we are cursed to stifle our creative instincts in order to participate in the tedium of that which has already been established in order to simply function as a coherent society, without actually contributing to that society in the manner we have evolved.

Still, despite this contradiction in human nature which forces us to balance risk with repression, there have been critical points in history wherein the very nature of human existence has been revolutionized. To reconcile this difference between the need to survive and the need to contribute to the survival of our species would represent such a revolution, allowing innovation, itself, to become the cornerstone of our basic survival skills, rather than hunting or manufacturing. Each new revolution advanced human ability to create and use new tools, and those innovations have, in turn, inspired new creativity. Within this dynamic lies the implications of a new revolution—one of aspiration—in which the driver of future growth is exactly that which has made humans uniquely adept at thriving among earth's creatures.

Each generation tends to resent the next, labeling them as entitled or lazy or otherwise not as good as their own. It is, in their view, audacious for these people now entering the workforce to demand a living wage that may seem high in terms of what the current generation believes they are earning relative to their knowledge and experience, but by modern price indices equals nothing more than an equivalence to what the current generation made when they first started working. To them, it is unthinkable that there should be so many people still filled with inspiration and aspiration when they, themselves, have already faced the hard reality that the current economic paradigm prevents the vast majority of people from realizing their dreams. It is believed that only by chance or by nepotism can anyone within the next generation experience success at an earlier age or with less experience. The things which are learned through experience and years of hard work are passed on and yet the new generation is accused when they learn from the past rather than trying to reinvent the wheel for themselves. It is thought that since the new generation is yet to acquire a piece of current knowledge, this, for some reason, makes it incomprehensible that they should have some new knowledge lacked by the previous generations. This is the nature of innovation, though. Each person has their own unique set of knowledge, and when bits of these knowledge sets are shared, as each person incorporates new ideas into their current knowledge set, it allows them to understand that knowledge within a new context, consider new applications for that knowledge, and use these new applications to improve upon old methods.

At the Center for Women's Entrepreneurship in Chatham University, executive director Rebecca Harris strongly advocates for a dynamic of learning she dubs "two-way mentoring", saying that young people should, "Find an established business leader who will take you under her wing. In return, she'll benefit from your social media and tech savvy."

It is the current generation which shapes the next, though, and sets the stage for them to either succeed by passing on the current knowledge so that it can be applied in new ways, or fail by assuming they are not capable of ingenuity. We live in an age established by innovation and the aspirations of bold and daring people. If these people waited until a time when they knew all that there was to know in order to take chances, then no chances would ever be taken, because we never truly know everything there is to know. It is in the nature of taking a chance that we are never fully ready, or else there would be nothing left to chance. This is the idea which built our world. We are now in a position to develop the economic structures necessary to both nurture this process, and to truly tap into its potential.

In order to accomplish this, though, we must encourage the public to use those things which make humans uniquely adept at functioning in this world. People must be given the opportunity and resources necessary to achieve the actualization of their aspirations in order to generate the kind of knowledge and innovation necessary for revolutionary progress to occur. As people, we cannot escape our need to develop and apply abstract principles for the purpose of creating solutions to our problems any more than birds can escape their need to annually migrate for the purpose of solving their own problems. The difference is that while birds work to solve the same problem constantly, we work to find and solve new problems, so that we have advanced to a point once thought impossible. The future is equally "impossible", and we can achieve it only if we create the structures in which people can utilize the skills available to them.

PROFILE: DON MUPSEY

Sometimes things do not work quite the way they were intended. For an entire lifetime he heard nothing but: "If you work hard and graduate from college, you will get a good job." So, that is what he did. He was accepted to a satisfactory university and joined the MBA program as a finance major. Finance was a respectable career field with growing opportunities, it seemed, and while working on his degree he worked for several companies to pay his bills and to learn how finances are managed in a variety of different industries. His life was going exactly as planned—complete an education, get a long-term career with a stable company, and start a family. All very typical—it was everything he was told life was supposed to be about. It was the American dream for his generation.

Like so many, though, he failed to learn from past generations that what he was being told was a dream, was nothing more than a dream. Reality was somehow much more distasteful, yet much more satisfying. Don graduated with an MBA in Finance, with honors, in the early months of 2008. He had already recognized in October 2007 that things were going wrong in the financial sector, and there was nothing that could be done about it, but in a way it was for the best. By this point he had recognized that it was not within him to be satisfied with the doldrums of menial office work (nor could he compete for entry-level positions with people that had 20 years of experience before getting laid off), and it had become entirely clear that the mainstream financial sector was about as respectable as the black market for counterfeit Rolex watches. Every direction he looked, it was a professional apocalypse, but that was ok—he had seen the Mad Max movies lots of times. This just meant finding his own way through the crumbling infrastructure and corrupt cannibals of what was once an economic empire, and becoming independently employed. He had better professional skills than most, so it was just a matter of finding customers.

This was entirely satisfying in a manner of speaking. People needed help understanding how to navigate the shambles of the financial world, so there was no shortage of customers with small projects who needed help finding their way back to normal operations. They were not long-term careers, and they did not pay well since the economy was in shambles, but he was doing something meaningful that really helped people—representing an industry that had destroyed itself in the way he thought it would when he first started college. With experience, and with challenges overcome, came questions, though. Questions about the nature of business, about the nature of people, about the nature of finance—all questions without answers. Finding the answers to these questions would give the world new knowledge, and in some cases would provide groundbreaking discoveries, and so Don became practically obsessed with the pursuit of research. By pushing the boundaries of human understanding and creating value that had no comparable alternative, Don had found a deeper purpose that contributed to the advancement of humanity—it utilized those processes that make humans unique to help ensure the continued progress of the species. Still, research paid even less than consulting. At least in consulting there were people willing to pay for assistance, but in research he found a meaningful pursuit for which no one asked and for which no one was paying. Combining the two paths earned enough money to live a certain kind of lifestyle—sharing a one-room apartment with a couple of roommates in the areas of town known for having higher rates of crime, drug use, and high school dropouts.

There was just one problem. Part of the original plan was to start a family, and this he had already done; gotten married and had several children. The career path he had pursued, despite having years of experience and a high degree of expertise, could not financially support a family. They were happy together—the kind of couple that others envied because they were so compatible yet did not flaunt it in public—and their children were thoughtful and well behaved (most of the time). That should have been purpose enough for one to have in their life, and so long as a job paid enough to sustain the family then that should be enough. Having spent a lifetime pursuing one career path, though, Don did not know how to do anything else that would pay any better. He could not be a computer programmer or a physician or a lawyer, even though those jobs were widely available, because he did not know how to do those things. Working in fast food or other consumer service jobs would not pay any better than he was already earning. So, even if he could mentally let go of an entire lifetime of dedication to mastering a specific field and find satisfaction doing other work for the sake of supporting his family, there were no viable options available. The only choice was to find a way to make more money pursuing his sense of purpose in life.

As of writing this, Don's struggle continues. Like the majority of Americans, his family is constantly on the verge of financial disaster—just one misstep or unfortunate circumstance from homelessness. Yet, he continues to work constantly, upward of 95 hours per week, just to try and keep paying the bills. It pays little, but they take solace in the knowledge that it is work that matters, and will have a lasting impact on the world, and just maybe it will pay off in their lifetime so that the struggle can end.

BIBLIOGRAPHY

Boomgaard, K. (2016, February 09). *Living right: Young entrepreneurs.* Retrieved April 08, 2017, from http://www.9and10news.com/story/31179170/living-right-young-entrepreneurs

Jelbert, S. A., Taylor, A. H., Cheke, L. G., Clayton, N. S., & Gray, R. D. (2014). Using the aesop's fable paradigm to investigate causal understanding of water displacement by new caledonian crows. *PLoS ONE, 9*(3). doi:10.1371/journal.pone.0092895.

CHAPTER 3

The Pursuit of Income

First of all, let us state the obvious: Being poor sucks. People have a lot of incentive to stop being poor, but very little opportunity. What the majority of people do not realize, though, is that everyone is in the pursuit of income—it is the very nature of human existence that our survival depends on the pursuit of an income-generating career—and yet when people do not have the opportunity to earn that which they have pursued then it harms the potential for everyone, including those who have had the opportunities to generate income.

There are all sorts of proverbs encouraging people to accept the idea that simply trying harder to not be poor is enough. We say things like "hard work brings success" and "success is 99% perspiration and 1% inspiration". The implication of this mindset is that poor people must be inherently immoral—lazy or degenerate—because they would be wealthy if they just worked harder and provided more value to society. For many, this doctrine of the immoral poor has gone as far as to become religious dogma. Starting sometime during the Middle Ages (prior to the rise of Martin Luther in 1517, but after the Council of Epaone in 517) it became popular for those who could afford it to simply pay the church to forgive their sins in a practice known as "Paying for Indulgences". Since the Catholic Church had, until that point, allowed people to provide services and do other works in exchange for the sins as a form of transaction, the philosophical implication of paying for indulgences was that those who were wealthy were simply entitled to sin. This religious philosophy continues today in something known as prosperity theology, which maintains that wealth is god's reward

© The Author(s) 2017
M. Taillard, *Aspirational Revolution*,
DOI 10.1007/978-3-319-61771-8_3

for living a more virtuous life, and that those who are poor suffer by their own sinful lifestyle of slothful depravity. The idea that being poor inherently makes you a bad person is very strongly ingrained in global cultures, from the (officially outlawed) caste system in India to the "bootstrap" culture of the United States, this poses a very serious barrier to any attempts people might make to improve their financial status.

For anyone who has actually been poor, however, and lived among peers who were poor, it is obvious that the reality is very different. The very idea is merely a dismissal and dehumanization of the poor in order to justify that what is happening is acceptable, despite the proven fact that only about 2% of benefits recipients are fraud cases, that the majority of homeless people only remain homeless for a few weeks, and that the nation's economy is entirely dependent on people who are not rich. Still, it has been built into the global economic infrastructure that those who are poor simply do not have the same opportunities to earn an income. The matter is complicated—very complicated—and nowhere is this better illustrated than in the financial sector, itself, through lending markets. It is here that something exists that is very obvious but seems to have gone completely unnoticed, which I call The Paradox of Credit. Rich or poor, this paradox has a negative effect on the daily lives of everyone, so pay close attention. We are going to look at it from the perspective of the lender and then the borrower. Here is how it goes:

Lenders give people money with the expectation that the money will be repaid with an additional amount equivalent to a percentage of the loan amount, called interest. Well, as a lender, before you give anyone money, you will want to assess whether or not the person asking to borrow money is likely to repay you in full and on time. This is usually done by checking a variety of factors, including a person's credit score (usually FICO), their recent income history, and so forth. No matter how credible the borrower appears to be, there is always a degree of uncertainty that the money will be repaid—perhaps a very reliable borrower has their own financial crisis and goes bankrupt. As a lender, this risk is just a cost of doing business; if people do not repay their loans, then you have lost money, incurring a cost. As a result, risk is treated as a cost. Using statistical analysis estimating the probability that a borrower will not repay their loan, they can determine the average risk cost that person represents. People who are much more likely to repay their loans represent a much lower risk cost, whereas those who are less likely to repay their loans represent a higher risk cost. It is for this reason that the interest rates between people will vary, and in a manner of speaking it is totally justified. If a product or service costs more to offer, then the producer must charge a higher price; in terms of loans, that means the lender must charge a higher interest rate if a borrower is statistically more likely to fail to repay their loans. Within the financial sector, this is an unquestionable fact—in order to make-up for the higher costs associated with high-risk loans, a higher interest rate must be charged.

From the perspective of a borrower, this logic has an obvious flaw. If the lender charges higher interest rates, then the borrower must pay higher monthly bills. These higher monthly bills make it more difficult for people to repay their loans, making it more likely that they will need to default on the loan. That is where the paradox exists: Lenders charge higher prices to borrowers who are statistically more likely to default, but by charging higher prices the lenders are directly making those borrowers more likely to default. It becomes a self-fulfilling prophecy in which no one wins. The lenders lose money because they are not repaid, yet the borrowers lose money because they must default on their loans, thereby likely having some of their things (homes, vehicles, etc.) repossessed so that the lender can auction it in the hopes of getting at least a portion of their money back.

To get all "economisty" for a moment, this paradox is actually quite profound when you start talking about monetary policy, because during a recession it is the standard response of central banks to make more money available for lending, thinking that it will stimulate economic growth. No, we are not talking about printing more money (not usually, anyway), because there are lots of better tools available to make that happen, and by using those tools the idea is that increasing the availability of money for lending it will encourage lenders to provide additional loans that increase demand for capital. The problem is that, during a recession, people do not have jobs, companies are not making money, and investors are looking for stability in the form of gold and government debt rather than pursuing new ventures or anything else that will contribute to economic stimulus. That means lending is much lower quality—there are fewer loans being issued because there are fewer companies that are expanding their operations and fewer people who can afford to repay a loan, and the loans which are issued during these time periods are of a higher risk than they normally would be just by nature of the volatile economic conditions. As a result, not only does this approach to economic stimulus through monetary policy do less to stimulate growth than it does contribute to liquidity traps, but by pushing lenders to issue loans of lower quality, there is a high likelihood that those loan assets will be overvalued in the long-run, which will necessitate their value eventually come back down in something called a "correction".

So, what does any of this have to do with the pursuit of income? Everything, actually. As the need to pursue income increases (i.e., lower levels of income), opportunities disappear. Expounding on the example of credit and lending, for those who make lower levels of income it is bad enough that each purchase they make consumes a greater percentage of their total income, but those purchases become even more expensive because of higher interest rates. So, rather than being able to pay for things in cash, or at very low interest rates, they must pay more for their purchases than the items they buy are actually worth. By the time a car loan, mortgage, even simple credit card debt is paid-off, a person has paid far more than the market value of the things they bought, which means they have paid far more for those things than someone who earns enough income to pay in cash. Moving on, with lower rates of income, simple subsistence living consumes the vast majority of a person's available finances (a concept called marginal propensity to consume (MPC), which is discussed in greater detail in Chap. 5), so they are generally incapable of allocating any of their money toward income-generating investments. Unlike those with higher income, who are able to use their money for financially constructive purposes of earning additional income through investing, people who earn lower rates of income do not have that option, particularly since the money they do have left over after paying for subsistence is most often used to pay interest costs to those who can use their money to issue debt investments. So, when a person does not have money, they never learn how to do things like invest, leaving them unable to teach their kids how to do these things, so that financial skills are not passed down through the generations. As a result, these families cannot afford to shop at the same stores, or attend the same social functions, or go to the same schools, live in the same areas, or otherwise network with people who do have opportunities and financial skills, creating a clear social divide in which opportunities to thrive simply do not exist for the majority of people.

To speak broadly, being poor sucks because it causes tremendous stress, because it causes people to be under the constant threat of losing one's home, family, or job. When the economy is doing poorly, low-income individuals are the first to lose their jobs and then compete with each other for what little work is available. Even during times of economic success, low-income individuals are still the first to lose their jobs to investments in automation which can perform the low-skill systematic labor more cheaply, thereby increasing the profitability of the businesses in which high-income people have invested. This suppresses the increases in income that would naturally occur during times of higher production and high employment demand. For the majority of the nation, there is that ever-present threat that their job will be replaced with automation, or sent to low-income nations, or otherwise just eliminated. Since the majority of the nation does not have financial security, it causes elevated levels of distress given that losing their job would have devastating results on their lives and the lives of their families. It has been demonstrated in multiple studies using both animals and people that when placed in a position of competition during a time of shortage, violence toward each other increases, and this crime causes further hardship. Merely the perception of shortage, whether it exists or not, will create elevated levels of aggression between people, contributing to the persistence of poverty.

None of this is debated—the disappearing middle class, the record number of millionaires, and the huge volume of people who have dropped below the poverty line are all acknowledged as well known and easily referenced. A 2012 study by the Congressional Research Service very clearly shows that economic growth is stimulated when tax rates on the very rich are higher. This principle has come to be known by the National Economic Council as "The Buffett Rule", named after wealthy investor Warren Buffett, who regularly advocates for higher taxes on the extremely wealthy as a way to stimulate the economy. Note that a progressive tax does not mean increasing the tax rate on all the income earned by a person, but increasing the tax rate on income which exceeds a certain level. So, if Person A earns significantly less than Person B, the taxation might look like this:

Person A: $X taxed at 10%
Person B: $X taxed at 10% + $Y taxed at 15%

Wherein both people are taxed the same on $X income, but since Person B earns more income, anything in excess of X is taxed at the higher rate. The Buffett Rule would place a much higher income tax on billionaires. This would support economic stimulus, which, as already stated, has some legitimacy to it, but the issue runs deeper than that.

When people have more money, especially those people who spend the vast majority of what they earn (those with low income), they spend more money, and companies earn more revenues thereby growing in size, increasing the value of the investments people make. It depletes surplus inventories, forcing companies to increase production, increasing the demand for more labor and increasing workers' opportunities to demand higher income. When people have the opportunity to earn a living wage, they are also able to save money and make investments, thereby generating more income, and this all causes the amount of government spending on assistance goes down. The average person receiving government financial assistance has some college education, is aged 30–40, and works at least full-time (often taking multiple jobs) but wages are too low to sustain the cost of living, so they must apply for benefits. When people have the opportunity to earn a living wage, the amount of spending on those benefits go down because people become self-reliant—the very thing that wealth-based philosophies try to accomplish.

By contrast, when people do not have the opportunity to pursue a proper income, the socioeconomic disparity grows (discussed further in Chap. 5), causing both the tax base and the consumer base to disappear. When people do not have money, they do not spend money, so companies are not making any revenues and must fire people and sell their assets to reduce production capacity and reduce costs in a self-perpetuating cycle of economic failure. Investors will not stop this because they are pulling their assets and investing them in safe havens like government debt, which will be in ample supply. When people and companies are not making money, then the government is not making any tax revenues, leading to increased reliance on debt to fund operations. The government can only raise tax rates so high on any group or transaction before people will stop paying it—either the money will simply not be available to pay or people will simply refuse. This is illustrated in something called the Laffer curve (an example of which is shown below in Fig. 3.1). When people cannot earn a proper income, there are fewer people who are able to pay taxes, requiring either a tax increase on those who are able or a reliance on government debt.

This is all fine, but what does the actual data say? According to a comprehensive Harvard Study, roughly two-third of people born to middle-income households stay there, and the income of a child born into a family at the top 90% of earners is expected to be roughly 300% higher than the income of a child born into a family at the bottom 10% of earners. Another study published in 2014 by a variety of economists from Harvard and the University of California showed that there was only about an 8.4% chance of someone born into poverty to make their way out of that cycle. It is much easier for someone in the top 1% to fall from their ranks than it is for someone in the bottom 10% to work their way up, yet losing one's status in

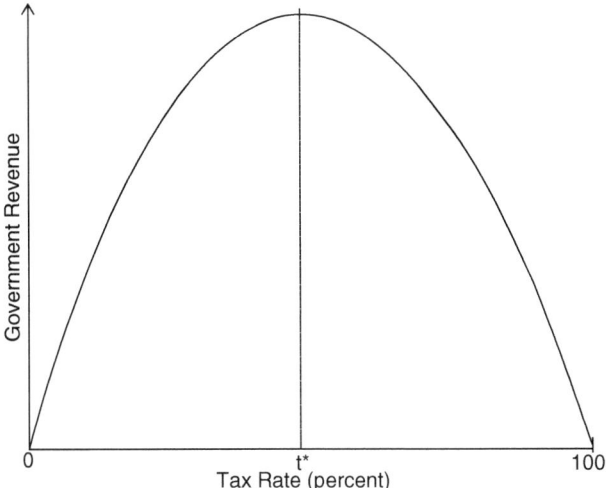

Fig. 3.1 Laffer curve

the top 1% still leaves them with a tremendous amount of wealth—not a middle-wage household, at all.

All the things we have discussed in this chapter work together to form a problem for the entire nation. The solution to which we so often turn is for the government to provide services. Many of the benefits programs available today are the result of The New Deal established under Franklin Roosevelt (seen as an expansion upon the Square Deal programs enacted by Teddy Roosevelt), which is credited with ending the Great Depression. These programs were developed and expanded by both major political parties who, at the time, recognized their function not only as treatment to what was seen as a humanitarian crisis, but also as an economic mechanism to correct the broken economic structure of the time. Since then, though, people in both major political parties have forgotten the original reasons for this, and many of these programs have been eroded or eliminated.

The truth is that many of these programs should be eliminated, but not for the reasons people seem to think. Using an entirely new economic paradigm, these programs become unnecessary and redundant, but to how can we be certain people will utilize this new paradigm? While this chapter has so far explained that it is almost impossible to stop being poor, and that poverty hurts the nation as a whole, it has yet failed to really elaborate on the original thesis that being poor sucks. Understanding why being poor sucks is the first and most important step in understanding why people pursue income. There are a variety of reasons that people want to work, and the pursuit of income is not the least of those reasons, but if the pursuit of income does not provide opportunity, as we have already established, then it can only be to avoid poverty.

To properly illustrate this point, let us look at one of the fundamentals of motivational theory: Maslow's Hierarchy of Needs (Fig. 3.2).

Looking at the pyramid, Maslow describes the things that people need to achieve in order of importance to be motivated. First, clearly, people need to meet their physiological needs; they need to have food, water, clothing, shelter, and so forth. Once they are assured their survival will continue, then they will worry about keeping their survival intact, by achieving their safety needs. That includes physical, financial, and social safety and stability. Having taken care of their most basic needs, people will seek more personal needs to find motivation, looking for social connections between coworkers and family, and trying to find pride in what they do. Finally, at the top of the pyramid, is self-actualization, which means the pursuit of your own ideas or passions and seeing them realized.

Well, when we compare Maslow's pyramid to the living conditions of the Great Depression, as mentioned earlier, it provides some amazing insight into why it sucks so badly to be poor. Without any income, you eliminate

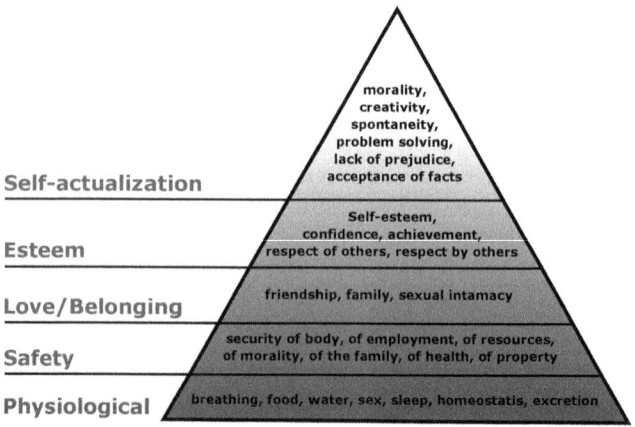

Fig. 3.2   Maslow's Hierarchy of Needs

very important things not only for your own survival, but for the survival of your family and children for whom you are obligated to care. During the Great Depression there were vast increases in the number of people who did not have access to food, so that soup lines were overburdened; and an increase in the number of people without homes, so that shanty-towns known as Hoovervilles made of scrap were built in public areas by those seeking even the most basic form of shelter. Disease was rampant during this time, with overcrowding, poor sanitation, and a lack of clean sources of water. A person's survival instinct is a very strong thing, and when the survival of a person or their family is threatened, they become desperate, so this was also a time of very high crime and struggle.

This situation was frequently abused, and contractors would visit these places with offerings of jobs, knowing entirely well that there would be competition for them. It was for that reason that these jobs were offered for nearly nothing—just enough money to get through the day—and frequently these jobs required people to pursue their physiological needs by ignoring their safety needs, as these jobs frequently involved unsafe machinery or dangerous working conditions. Workplace deaths and injuries during this time were high. So, given conditions such as that, it should come as no surprise that people have a strong drive to pursue income, and there is indisputable evidence that, in fact, they do.

Although policy has lessened the severity with which people face many of these issues, they persist even today. As we will discuss in more detail throughout the remainder of this book, real wages (wages adjusted for increases in the cost of living) have not increased for the vast majority of people since the nation recovered from the Great Depression, and it is in the nature of the labor markets that the majority of people still desperately compete with each other over jobs which only meet the minimum necessities for survival, and most of the time for safety. Without opportunity to achieve more, and without opportunity to increase real wages, the pursuit of income does not come from a passion for one's work, but rather the need to prevent poverty (this will be discussed in more detail in Chap. 5).

It is because being poor sucks that most people are not willing to pursue professional risk. This is referring to the amount of risk inherent in pursuing the top tiers of Maslow's pyramid—in pursuing innovation and creation. Most people pursue traditional work because it is safer, or because they know of no other way to survive. As a result our society fails to benefit from the potential these people have, the ideas they hold, the inventions and research they could provide, the free market competition they could inspire.

How many Van Goghs or Teslas have we lost because it sucks to be poor? By creating a new economic paradigm, the pursuit of income and the pursuit of purpose can be aligned, eliminating the struggle that we, as humans, must face.

Profile: Ty William

Ty's story is a short one with a happy ending, but which includes taking a hell of a risk in the pursuit of income. It is not uncommon for people who speak English as a native language to travel overseas to teach English, and China is one of the more common destinations. As long as you have a four-year degree in any topic, you can take up work on a "foreign expert" visa. For the schools, it is a status symbol to have a foreign teacher who is a native English speaker lead the language courses, which is why Ty's first trip to China was on a contract of RMB 8000 per month (which is roughly average for these contracts). At the time, that would have been roughly $1000 per month, which is quite a bit more than Chinese teachers make, and vastly more than supporting staff. The important thing to remember is a little thing called purchasing power parity, which basically means stuff in China is a lot cheaper to buy, so that RMB 8000 per month would provide a decent, middle-income living comparable to the United States, particularly once you take into account the fact that most of these teaching contracts include rent-free apartments, free food (if you do not mind eating at the school cafeteria), and travel reimbursement at the end of your contract. Ty's experience was one that is fairly typical for English teachers in China—a bit of money, some fun and travel, and an overall enjoyable experience.

It was only his first trip that went smoothly, however. After a bad breakup and dropping-out of law school, he felt the need to run . . . it did not matter where, so long as he was far away from those things which vexed him, so he accepted the first contract he found to teach on the opposite side of the planet. He was lucky. After his contract expired, he returned to the United States and decided he wanted to pursue a career teaching, enrolled in a master's program to get certified, then decided he preferred teaching in China. This time he approached his trip in a more haphazard manner. He only knew he needed a career teaching, and he was back in China. This time the schools at which he taught were not so typical. They paid poorly and had poor working conditions—he was a stranger in a foreign land not making enough income to survive, not enough money to travel home, and switching between schools desperately trying to find something credible.

Overconfidence led to carelessness and poor planning, which was his own fault, but at that moment the cause did not matter—he needed a solution.

It was only by luck that that he stumbled across the school SAS, which he did not know at the time was considered among the best in Asia, and that they just happened to be looking for an English teacher with a master's degree. The Chinese would have called it an auspicious event. He stayed with them for two years making a more typical salary for a native English speaker, and it was during this time he became aware of all the schools which tried to lure foreign teachers for unreasonably low wages. He received many offers during that time from schools similar to those "shitty" ones at which he had taught before, providing perspective on the nature of the market and just how many teachers must get suckered into these positions (or maybe it was just his own recklessness). Even at SAS, he was making a living, but not making enough money for a true career. It was still more akin to those experiences for foreign English teachers who want to teach in China for one or two years and then go somewhere else, probably back to their home nation. For someone looking to make a lifelong career out of it, this still was not enough.

It is in the nature of teaching English in China, though, that if you have the proper credentials and last more than two years that you will eventually get the attention of one of the major international schools. In Ty's case, he was recruited by the International School of Beijing to work at their Shanghai location, earning roughly $3\times$ the amount an English teacher would make in the United States. For Ty there is no longer a pursuit of income. He has overcome that hurdle, and now focuses on the pursuit of his passion—teaching English to those students who struggle most.

BIBLIOGRAPHY

2016 Federal Tax Rates, Personal Exemptions, and Standard Deductions. (n.d.). Retrieved April 08, 2017, from https://www.irs.com/articles/2016-federal-tax-rates-personal-exemptions-and-standard-deductions

Chetty, R., Hendren, N., Kline, P., & Saez, E. (2014). Where is the land of opportunity? The geography of intergenerational mobility in the United States. *The Quarterly Journal of Economics.* doi:10.3386/w19843

Chetty, R., Grusky, D., Hell, M., Hendren, N., Manduca, R., & Narang, J. (2016). The fading American dream: Trends in absolute income mobility since 1940. doi:10.3386/w22910

Hoovervilles and Homelessness. (n.d.). Retrieved April 08, 2017, from http://depts.washington.edu/depress/hooverville.shtml

Hoovervilles During the Great Depression – American Memory Timeline-Classroom Presentation | Teacher Resources. (n.d.). Retrieved April 08, 2017, from http://www.loc.gov/teachers/classroommaterials/presentationsand activities/presentations/timeline/depwwii/depress/hoovers.html

Hungerford, T. L. (2012). *Taxes and the economy: An economic analysis of the top tax rates since 1945.* Washington, DC: Congressional Research Service.

Lollar, D. (1974). An operationalization and validation of the Maslow need hierarchy. *Educational and Psychological Measurement, 34*(3), 639–651. doi:10.1177/001316447403400316

Staff, I. (2012, November 07). *Buffett rule.* Retrieved April 08, 2017, from http://www.investopedia.com/terms/b/buffettrule.asp

CHAPTER 4

The Pursuit of Passion

While it is true that everyone needs to eat to survive, an offering of bread and water is not enough to fan the flames of passion for one's work. To extend the conversation from Chap. 2, perhaps it is all in the name: Maslow was only looking at our needs as individual people. As we will discuss in Chap. 6, though, the nature of what it even means to be human has changed over time—the methods by which we acquire our needs has changed dramatically since the Stone Age. In modern society—one dominated by the cooperative production of goods you do not personally need so that you can trade them for the things you do—motivation is driven not by the pursuit of food, because food is now acquired by pursuing employment. As a result, motivation is a critical feature to our survival, and nothing motivates a person like the opportunity to pursue something for which they have a burning passion.

Perhaps we have been looking at Maslow's Pyramid of Needs all wrong. Not everyone feels the need to establish safety or esteem in their careers, and, in extreme cases, some people are not even concerned with the physiological needs. At the bottom of the pyramid, the physiological needs, we find the things which are in greatest abundance, though—they are the easiest to achieve. The majority of people who pursue traditional work simply to survive will be able to find it—there are enough jobs or other roles a person can pursue that fulfill these needs. Those who pursue traditional work simply attempting to survive, however, will find it most difficult to climb that pyramid to meet higher-level needs.

© The Author(s) 2017
M. Taillard, *Aspirational Revolution*,
DOI 10.1007/978-3-319-61771-8_4

Consider it another way by looking at someone who pursues their aspirations despite the risk; the person who forgoes regular work so that they might do something for which they have a passion, or which they feel has great importance. In other words, let us flip the pyramid upside-down. Just as the bottom of the pyramid is now the smallest, so too will far fewer people who pursue self-actualization as their primary goal succeed in their endeavors. It is extremely difficult to find success in these fields, which is why we have tropes such as the "starving artist". By pursuing work primarily for having a sense of pursuing one's purpose in life, they will find it easier to achieve self-actualization and esteem, but these pursuits often come with little or no income—climbing the inverted pyramid means working with a purpose while attempting to find ways to make money doing it.

Maslow's Pyramid, then, can be translated as something entirely different. Its original purpose of illustrating what people need to find motivation fails in that such things as income do not function well as motivators. People will seek them out of necessity, but they do not push people to excel. Instead, we can look at it as an illustration of opportunity. There are fewer opportunities to achieve esteem and self-actualization through one's professional life, but they provide greater drive to achieve great things. The risk inherent in pursuing such work, though, drives people who pursue those professional paths which have greater volumes of opportunity to meet basic survival needs, working their entire lives in that path at the risk of spending a lifetime in a role of professional mediocrity.

In any case, it is quite clear that people want to work. The idea that people would sit on the couch constantly doing nothing if given the opportunity is a myth. People need to feel as though they have purpose, the only question—the only thing that changes from person to person—is the nature of that purpose. Each person is motivated by different things, and if their professional needs are not being met in their current role, they will fail to thrive—fail to meet their full potential. Still, people would rather work a poor job, or attempt to make a fulfilling career on their own, than do nothing at all. According to Johns Hopkins Medical Center, inactivity causes anxiety and depression, naturally leading to higher rates of suicide and other self-destructive behavior. Inactivity also causes physical harm, such as high blood pressure and heart disease, leading to long-term medical complications and higher costs associated with healthcare. Simply put, people are instinctually driven to remain active in order to maintain their health and sanity.

In order to illustrate the dynamics between wages and purpose in the workplace, artist Blake Fall-Conroy developed something he calls a Minimum Wage Machine. It looks a bit like a wooden gumball machine filled with pennies, and has a hand crank on the side. A person will stand there and turn the crank, and the machine will dispense one penny every few seconds, so that the rate of pay is equal to the minimum wage. Theoretically, a person could stand at the machine for a 40-hour workweek and earn a minimum wage living, but they do not. According to Fall-Conroy, a typical two-month long showing would pay-out roughly $20 worth of pennies.

The math on that is simple:

The US federal minimum wage is $7.25 per hour. The number of weeks in a month varies a bit, but given roughly four weeks in a month, that means the machine was only used for 2.76 hours over the course of eight weeks. A typical full-time job requires 40 hours of work each week, for a total of 320 hours over the same eight-week period. So, although a person could earn minimum wage, or people could even wait in line and take turns so that the machine was continuously paying minimum wage, the idea of being paid for something so pointless was so unbearable that there was a 99.14% rate of underutilized labor.

One might make the argument that the lack of use of the minimum wage machine was the result of the fact that people simply do not want to work. To address this, let us take this concept to the real world, and look to the US automotive industry. The world-renowned "Big 3" included Ford, General Motors, and Chrysler; but by the late twentieth century they all found themselves struggling to compete against foreign auto manufacturers from Japan, South Korea, India, Germany, Italy, and others. There just was not as much demand for sales from the Big 3 anymore, and so sales volume dropped. The consequence of lower demand was that these companies did not need the same degree of production capacity anymore, which meant using fewer workers. Due to agreements with the United Auto Workers (the automotive labor union), they could not simply remove workers from their jobs, however, so rather than continuing to produce the same volume of cars at overcapacity, they paid the employees to do nothing. It was a program called the Jobs Bank, and employees that were not needed were offered 95% of their pay to do nothing. If someone in the program was offered work within the company within an 80-mile radius of their home, then they had to take it or else get eliminated from the company completely. One might think that this would have been a popular program among workers since they were getting paid to do nothing, but as we have already established, people need to feel a sense of purpose. At the height of the layoffs in 2006, the Jobs Bank included roughly 15,000 people, but the reality of getting paid to do nothing was so miserable that within two years the number of people participating was a mere 3500. Note that 2008 was also the year of the financial collapse—a period in which banks and auto-motive manufacturers alike were laying-off people and begging the govern-ment for help. So, the Jobs Bank program was so intensely unpopular that it lost 75% of its participants in two years, despite increasing volumes of people who would have qualified for the program. For those who were in the program, instead of sitting around doing nothing, they decided to go out and do community service. Even being given the option of contributing positively to the community was not enough, however, because people have professional needs. I reiterate: People want to work!

So, since people were leaving the Jobs Bank program, what did people do instead? Some of them had met the qualifications for an early retirement, and decided to take that route. Early retirements are a typical part of the labor market, however, so this came as no surprise. The vast majority of them, though, went-on to find different jobs. Rather than get paid to do nothing, and rather than get paid to volunteer in the community, they decided to leave their company to find different work.

So, even when people have the opportunity to earn money, they will leave it quickly unless it gives them some sort of sense of purpose and professional fulfillment. That is where Herzberg's Two-Factor Theory of motivation becomes relevant (Fig. 4.1).

Notice that the potential benefits of a particular job are split into two categories of factors. Hygiene factors are those things which people need in order to make the job minimally tolerable for the majority of people. This stuff includes most of the things in the bottom two levels of Maslow's Pyramid, and maybe a few things in the third level. These are the things which will allow most people to keep a job, but they will not thrive—they will not be driven. By contrast, there are motivational factors, and these are the things which inspire employees to really push for improved productivity. These are the things found at the top levels of Maslow's Pyramid.

To give this concept a bit of validity, a 2010 study by Oswald, Proto, and Sgroi showed that there was a 12% increase in productivity when employees were happy. By contrast, they were also able to show that there was a 10% decrease in productivity from those who were unhappy (particularly from those who had experienced a recent event that caused them to be depressed). When I apply Herzberg's model to this data, it clearly

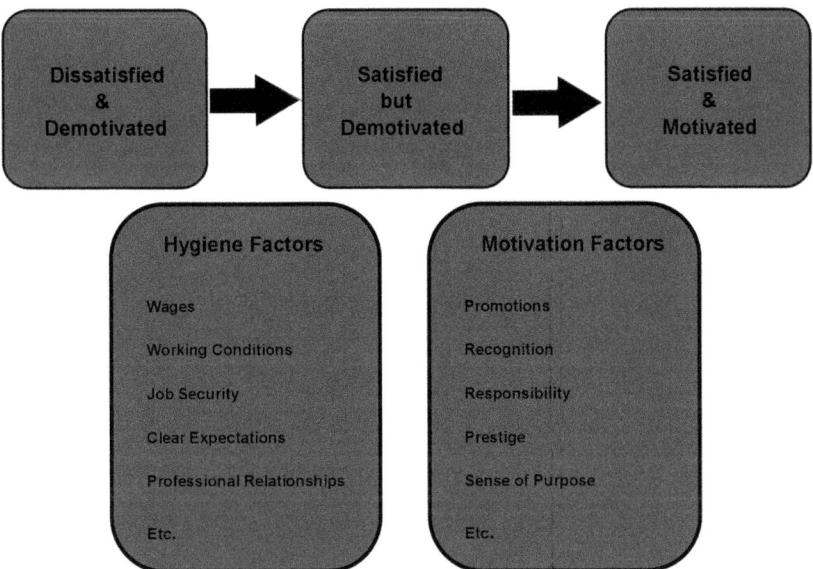

Fig. 4.1 Herzberg's Two-Factor Theory of motivation

demonstrates that when people have the opportunity to pursue their aspirations—when they are allowed to work toward a purpose in their life—it leads to a more efficient labor force. On the other hand, forcing people into tedious work that they hate simply because they need the money to meet their basic survival needs, and are under the constant threat of being replaced if they step out of line contributes to satisficing behavior in the labor force. Satisficing, by the way, is a behavioral economics term that means making decisions which are "good enough", rather than optimal. An unsatisfied workforce will maintain a production rate that is good enough to earn consistent wages, but will not be passionate about their work, resulting in a huge loss of national production potential. It should come as no surprise, then, when we talk about automation later in the book, how jobs are being replaced by technology at a faster rate due to differences in production efficiency.

Productivity is the result of a happy workforce, and people feel most happy when they are motivated. For too long people have been trying to find ways to motivate people to do anything, but no matter what incentives you provide, you simply will never truly motivate someone to turn a hand crank for minimum wage, or to sit in a room doing nothing. People are motivated when given the opportunity to pursue their inspirations. Usually people are inspired by their work—it is something they do every day, so it is natural that a person should find creativity in their work. Being allowed to pursue that—and in some cases even being allowed to spearhead projects, or giving recognition for their pursuits, is what truly motivates, according to Herzberg.

When people are motivated and they are passionate about what they do, it will show in the quality of their work, and eventually people will recognize it. Whether in a more traditional work setting in which a person is recognized and given responsibility over the success of a new project, or whether someone is foregoing a safe but mediocre career in the pursuit of their passion, people recognize the difference. This is important not just for the fulfillment of one's own professional needs, but it is important to customers that someone is giving them the highest standard of workmanship, and it is important to employers that someone is providing not only higher levels of productivity, but also innovative new ideas to improve the business.

Maslow said that we must first meet our baser needs before we can achieve upper-level needs, but the bottom of the pyramid is not wider because it is more important, but because there is more opportunity to fulfill those needs—it is simply easier. Is this truly living, though, or is it merely existing? If we produce so that we can consume, and then consume so that we can produce, then there is no opportunity for humanity to truly advance. Those who focus entirely on the bottom inherently cannot focus on achieving the more difficult levels of purpose, such as self-actualization. By focusing on the top of the pyramid and pursuing passions and purpose, it becomes possible to emphasize quality and innovation within the labor force. It is from this position that the lower levels of Maslow's pyramid become more accessible. By pursuing a passion, there is opportunity to develop one's own self-esteem, and the quality and motivation that such a person brings to their work will earn the esteem of others. The remainder of the pyramid (i.e., social, safety, and physiological needs) are met while finding opportunities to market one's pursuits, either to coworkers and employers to get approval, or to customers for the financial gains necessary to pay the bills. In either case, it is easier to focus on achieving the more difficult needs and let your passions provide opportunities to pay the bills, than it is to exclusively pursue payment in the hopes that working hard in a job which provides no satisfaction provide opportunities to meet higher-level needs.

It does not require one to be a lone, starving artist, foregoing more basic needs to pursue their passions. As stated earlier in this chapter, most people find passion in their work, but it must be work about which they are passionate. Labor mobility must be available, allowing people to more easily change jobs, change companies, or change locations, so that the labor force can optimally match skill sets with job requirements. This is a difficult transition for most, as it comes with the threat of losing the income they already have with no certainty of finding new income, but the implications are great. To facilitate this dynamic, a new macroeconomic paradigm must be established to make it more accessible to those who would not have otherwise taken the risk, regardless of how their ideas might revolutionize the world. It does not require one to be a lone, starving artist, either. As we will explore in later chapters, it is not singular large moments of revolution which drive human progress; it is small innovations with wider implications discovered initially by people who learned to improve their work by letting their passion drive them to learn more about it, and create new methods for accomplishing it.

The calculations supporting this are simple.

$$Productivity = Ability^*Motivation^*Environment$$

In other words, the amount of stuff a person can achieve in a productive workday is simply a matter of that person's ability (e.g., their experience, skill, knowledge, etc.), the environment in which they are working (i.e., which generally emphasizes the technology available to them, but also includes a variety of lesser factors such as organizational structure and so forth), and the degree to which that person is motivated. Now, motivation is what we have been talking about for a large percentage of this chapter; passion to drive people to thrive and excel in their work. The calculation for motivation proposed by Temporal Motivational Theory is:

$$Motivation = \frac{(Expectations^*Value)}{(1 + Impulsiveness^*Delay)}$$

In other words, as the value of an outcome increases and the degree to which a person expects that the outcome is likely increases, a person will be more motivated, but this will be tempered by a person's need to delay their gratification. This little equation actually summarizes our chapter quite nicely. If a person can pursue their passions at work—if they have the opportunity to pursue motivating factors instead of hygiene factors—then they will be more greatly driven to contribute their efforts and innovations. However, if that pursuit causes them to live in desperate poverty for an extended period of time, then the opportunity may pose the perception of greater risk than the person is willing to take. So, in our equation, if motivation is greater than 1, the person is motivated; and motivation is less than 1, the person is not motivated. Of course, these are all things which are subjective and if they are not impossible to measure, then they are at least impossible to predict. As a result, the equation functions more as a tool to illustrate the nature of motivation than provide a useful measurement tool. That is why we are using it to summarize the chapter, rather than trying to incorporate it earlier.

PROFILE: L. E. SALAS

Luis had been enthralled by filmmaking since childhood. For as long as he can remember, he has been inspired by the classic films of the 1980s and 1990s, but as a film student in college his interests shifted somewhat. His revelation came during his first documentary film course, in which he became aware that film could be used not just for artistic or entertainment purposes, but to make a tangible difference in the world. Suddenly, his original plans seemed superficial. Originally intending to network in the industry and write himself into film roles of increasing prominence, he became aware that film could be used to give people insight and perspective on important issues by entertaining them, requiring neither boring academic research nor lofty pretentious art.

Currently he has solid career plans with an important goal, but is finding it difficult to make them a reality. The goal is to open an "efficient and state of the art multimedia facility that would give pre-collegiate students who are interested, a more intense approach to TV and filmmaking". It is a new model of production and education within the industry. In a way, this facility would function to provide apprenticeships, creating documentaries and short films with intentions of full public distribution, while involving young people who want to train in a hands-on learning environment. His past films were created without the benefit of such a facility, yet have still garnered attention. His 2013 film Dead Man Working (a feature film that used the zombie apocalypse as an allegory for the issues surrounding migrant labor in the US) won Best Screenplay and Best Editing at the Hoboken Film Festival, despite having a tremendously low budget (he takes great pride in showing what he can accomplish under intense cost constraints). By running the planned facility, he and permanent staff starting at roughly ten people, would be able to continuously produce high-caliber documentary and shorts for film and television, and use the profits from those operations to fund periodic large productions of importance to current "cultural zeitgeist", all while training their pre-collegiate apprentices in every aspect of the industry.

Long-term plans include expanding the facility in order to handle more ambitious projects in greater volume. The impact on employment, by the very nature of the industry, would be quite variable. There would be an increasing number of permanent staff, contributing in a moderate way to the demand for workers with a variety of specialized skills, adding to the diversity of the skill sets in demand within the local area. Given the continuous cycle of apprenticeships being offered, that would also contribute to the volume of people able to pursue their own ventures in TV and film production, so that each apprentice eventually creates jobs by producing their own media, or offering their varied skill sets and contributing to the skill level and diversity of labor skills available within a distributed region. What makes this particular industry unique, however, is that each production filmed will require a variable number of people. One project might need only 50 people, while another might need 500. Also unique is the fact that at times these temporary workers will be on-site at the facility, and other times they would need to film at remote locations, which means that this variable rate of employment impact will be partially mobile, contributing to one area this year, and another area the next. Each filming cite, of course, will experience temporary increases in demand for supporting industries, primarily in hospitality (e.g., food, shelter, etc.). This unusual arrangement has a unique impact on economies in that they offer temporary stimulus of a variety of regions, while also functioning as a constant contribution to the economy of their headquarters.

As of now, these plans will never come to fruition, though. He has tried the path of the starving artist in the past, and found that it was "neither attractive nor a feasible option". He cites his age and current obligations as reasons why such a path is no longer an option, though calculations show that it is very unlikely that using this method would raise enough funds to open the facility in question, anyway. At any rate, he is not willing to take the risk, saying, "The biggest impediment in pursuing independent filmmaking as a start-up company would be leaving my comfortable, salary job; it is painfully comfortable." In order for this project to become feasible, he would need financial support from investors, possibly from a more established producer, or would otherwise require access to grants of some sort. He says that a grant would absolutely make a difference, making the facility possible in the immediate future, but that since such grants are practically nonexistent, he would need access to an amazing grant writer. Still, Salas holds on to hope that his ability to operate at such cost-efficient levels will be a key selling point for potential grantors. "I have kept most of my past independent projects at relatively low budgets. It is a practice I have been able to utilize outside of my full-time production job in order to attract potential producers with a demonstration of what can be done or how a project can look on a dramatically low budget, hoping they would be interested in taking up a level for a lager production."

BIBLIOGRAPHY

Hinton, B. L. (1968). An empirical investigation of the Herzberg methodology and two-factor theory. *Organizational Behavior and Human Performance, 3*(3), 286–309. doi:10.1016/0030-5073(68)90011-1

Langfitt, F. (2006, February 02). *Idled auto workers tap the jobs bank*. Retrieved April 08, 2017, from http://www.npr.org/templates/story/story.php?storyId=5185887

Minimum Wage Machine. (n.d.). Retrieved April 08, 2017, from http://www.blakefallconroy.com/18.html

Oswald, A., Proto, E., & Sgroi, D. (2015). Happiness and productivity. *Journal of Labor Economics, 33*(4) 789–822.

Risks of Physical Inactivity. (n.d.). Retrieved April 08, 2017, from http://www.hopkinsmedicine.org/healthlibrary/conditions/cardiovascular_diseases/risks_of_physical_inactivity_85,P00218/

CHAPTER 5

The Pursuit of Freedom

Freedom takes many forms, and for an economy to be truly prosperous, each of those forms must be exercised to their fullest. Not only must the people and resources of a nation be able to organize themselves in the manner most efficient, but they must be accessible, or have access, when there arises the opportunity to contribute in the manner which maximizes their potential. In its most foundational sense, the only restrictions of our freedom are those we place on ourselves. Each of us are free to pursue the actions we independently deem optimal, but within the context of a given social and economic structure, there are risks to every action, and risks to every inaction, which must be weighed prior to making the decision to exercise that freedom. Throughout history there have been structures which place great risk and cost on actions which deviate from expectations—those which violate a norm. Such extreme examples persist even today in those areas of the world torn asunder by the dominance of warlords, and those areas ruled via the totalitarian suppression of independent thought and expression. Even in these areas, though—even in the worst of times— each person has within them the freedom to act according to their own will, so long as they are willing to face those risks associated with their actions.

In a more civilized time and place the risks and costs associated with exercising freedoms tend to be less severe, yet they do persist in a more subtle form. As discussed in Chaps. 2 and 3, in the modern era people need an income to survive, and to forego this in the pursuit of greater ambitions poses the risk of being socially and economically banished from the means by which a person acquires the means of their subsistence. Yet freedom is

© The Author(s) 2017
M. Taillard, *Aspirational Revolution*,
DOI 10.1007/978-3-319-61771-8_5

critical to an efficient market, which means that it is vital to develop a structure in which we are facilitating the ability of workers to alter the nature of their labor contributions, known as labor mobility. In order to guarantee the proper matching of workers with particular skill sets with employers who are in demand of those specific skill sets, people must be free to move geographically; people must be free to change the company for which they work, or if such a company does not exist they must be free to start their own by means of entrepreneurship; people must be free to change jobs, or if such a job does not yet exist they must be free to create it by means of self-employment; people must be free to acquire skills and knowledge applicable to the markets, or if such skills and knowledge do not yet exist they must be free to explore beyond the yet undiscovered bounds of human understanding. These are the freedoms which must be available to all people to achieve true labor mobility—for the labor markets to be truly efficient. In order for a nation to successfully accomplish this, however, such a nation must adopt structures which facilitate these freedoms.

Regardless of what other risks might be imposed upon people who pursue mobility greater than the existing structures facilitate, the most omnipresent—the most persistent and common of those risks which might exist—is losing access to the resources necessary for subsistence. As discussed in Chap. 4, the pursuit of one's passion often means ending the pursuit of income, and if a person does not already own the resources to subsist during that time in which income is not being made, then life will be most difficult, indeed. This risk of extreme poverty and the hardships associated with it are not the natural result of market forces, but rather it is built into the social and economic structures which collude to shape the markets by conscious intention. This matter is addressed in *The Wealth of Nations*, Book 1 Chapter 8, Paragraph 13, in which Adam Smith states:

> We rarely hear, it has been said, of the combinations of masters, though frequently of those of workmen. But whoever imagines, upon this account, that masters rarely combine, is as ignorant of the world as of the subject. Masters are always and everywhere in a sort of tacit, but constant and uniform combination, not to raise the wages of labor above their actual rate. To violate this combination is everywhere a most unpopular action, and a sort of reproach to a master among his neighbors and equals. We seldom, indeed, hear of this combination, because it is the usual, and one may say, the natural state of things, which nobody ever hears of. Masters, too, sometimes enter into particular combinations to sink the wages of labor even below this rate.

These are always conducted with the utmost silence and secrecy, till the moment of execution, and when the workmen yield, as they sometimes do, without resistance, though severely felt by them, they are never heard of by other people. Such combinations, however, are frequently resisted by a contrary defensive combination of the workmen; who sometimes too, without any provocation of this kind, combine of their own accord to raise the price of their labor. Their usual pretenses are, sometimes the high price of provisions; sometimes the great profit which their masters make by their work. But whether their combinations be offensive or defensive, they are always abundantly heard of. In order to bring the point to a speedy decision, they have always recourse to the loudest clamor, and sometimes to the most shocking violence and outrage. They are desperate, and act with the folly and extravagance of desperate men, who must either starve, or frighten their masters into an immediate compliance with their demands. The masters upon these occasions are just as clamorous upon the other side, and never cease to call aloud for the assistance of the civil magistrate, and the rigorous execution of those laws which have been enacted with so much severity against the combinations of servants, laborers, and journeymen. The workmen, accordingly, very seldom derive any advantage from the violence of those tumultuous combinations, which, partly from the interposition of the civil magistrate, partly from the necessity superior steadiness of the masters, partly from the necessity which the greater part of the workmen are under of submitting for the sake of present subsistence, generally end in nothing, but the punishment or ruin of the ringleaders.

Though the term "wage slavery" has fallen out of favor, during the time of Adam Smith it was commonly used to succinctly refer to the dynamic described above. This is a dynamic which has not changed for hundreds of years, quite demonstrably since at least 1776 when the *Wealth of Nations* was originally published. The similarities to the Mohawk Valley Formula (a formalized method for breaking-up labor strikes developed and successfully utilized by the Remington Rand Company in 1936) are striking, as the steps to this formula explicitly include installing people among the ranks of labor unions to take violent or otherwise illegal actions, and encourage others among those desperate for income to do the same, so that the company might call upon law enforcement to break-up the strike. According to the formula, the strikers should then be portrayed to the public as a minority of discontented and inherently disruptive mobsters.

So, clearly it is not in the nature of companies, as a generalized sector of the economy, to raise wages beyond the levels necessary for bare subsistence of the workers, nor has it ever been their nature. Data from the US Congressional Budget Office (detailed further in this chapter) clearly shows that income for the vast majority of people has not increased at all since at least the early twentieth century, and has actually decreased relative both to the total productivity of the nation and to the total income earned by the nation as a whole. Complicating the matter is that there is often little or no incentive for a single employer to improve labor mobility and the pursuit of freedom—such things frequently benefit employers only as they benefit the nation as a whole. So, given the current structural paradigm of the economy, the dynamics of the labor market are not likely to change. We have built into our economic paradigm a structural propensity to trend toward inefficient use of labor. We have created a system in which the systematic prevention of peoples' pursuit of freedom must persist.

In one respect (and potentially only this one respect) there is merit to this structure. It is inefficient to distribute the resources for labor mobility to everyone just by some change that they will pursue it. Everyone participates in labor mobility, but it is only a small minority of people who are actively seeking mobility at any given moment. So, by making resources available for the purpose of mobility will primarily result primarily in an increase in consumer spending similar to a tax credit, or a legally obligated increase in wages (e.g., minimum wages). While these things do have their own functions, which will be discussed in the second half of this book, the function of these things is not to maintain an improvement in labor mobility.

The pursuit of freedom can be structurally facilitated not through the inefficiency of perpetual distribution of resources to all, at all times, but rather through more targeted means by which resources are made available to those with a comprehensive plan to mobilize. Such a structure, by the very nature of requiring a person to have a plan, would be a grant-based system through which resources are made available.

The current role of grants as a consistent tool within global economic paradigm, is limited. Grants are (almost) exclusively treated as contracts. Visiting the website Grants.gov (which is the website the US government uses to solicit bids for its grants) will quickly show you a list of grants being offered, all of them intended to tender some service, such as perform some specific study, coordinate specific events, organize or manage a specific program, and so forth. They are each driven by the needs of a single entity—the US government—and are typically only granted to existing and established organizations (as of writing this, only 2.49% of grants being solicited are available to individuals, most or all of which will be given in favor of existing and established organizations). For example, although the US Department of Justice has issued its annual grant to do a research and evaluation study on drugs and crime in the United States, historically these grants are given exclusively to large and well-established non-profit organizations dedicated to fighting the "war on drugs", or universities. That is just the current role of grants.

There are a comparatively small number of grants issued by government agencies and private institutions for unique purposes, such as community outreach programs, arts education, environmental revitalization, and so forth. There are a comparatively small volume of these, their total value is considerably less, and—as always—they are solicited for a specific service, making them function more like a contract than a true grant. These also tend to be less consistent, as non-profit expenditures fluctuate much more wildly with variations in the economy than other types of transactions. When a recession hits, non-profits tend to be hit first, and hit the hardest, yet it is during a recession when the most consideration needs to be made for economic stimulus and labor mobility. Thus, any structure facilitating the pursuit of freedom must function in a manner that is unique from the existing grant structures.

To improve the nation by facilitating the pursuit of freedom, the way in which resources are made available must be efficient, hence the need for a grant-based program that funds comprehensive plans that will improve the allocation of labor potential, but they must be responsive to the evolution of free market forces. Current programs to improve labor mobility help somewhat match workers with jobs in a very limited manner, but fail entirely in fulfilling the function of facilitating economic growth and development. It is not their fault that they fail to do this, because that was never their intended goal, since they were designed exclusively as matching services. These exist in both the public and private sectors. In the private sector there are temp agencies, which are hired by companies who need to hire people for only a limited period of time. From the perspective of the worker, moving from company to company through temp agencies can become a full-time career, though the available jobs tend to pay poorly since these services attract companies who need to fill roles that take little or no experience, and the agency needs take their percentage as well, in order to continue operating. There are also headhunting services, which is the term used for any general staffing service. These are companies who fulfill parts of the human

resources function for their client companies—finding people with particular skill sets, and screening them so that the company looking for employees
can more easily select someone qualified. From the government end, there
are similar services available wherein companies can list the jobs they need
filled on websites and/or at service centers. These have the same basic
function as the wanted ads in newspapers. There are programs which can
help people get a basic education, such as a General Educational Development Diploma (GED), to become qualified to perform certain jobs.

The primary program that helps to facilitate the pursuit of freedom,
rather than simply acting as a matching service, is the unemployment
insurance programs. Such programs help people who have lost their job
through no fault of their own (i.e., quitting, illegal activities, etc.) lost
their job. In other words, a mismatch of the supply and demand for their
particular skill set was created in the market, and the person must spend
their time finding a new match. This is unique in that it does provide
financial funding for the person to pursue an improvement in labor
market efficiency by whatever means they see possible. Should the person
choose to pursue something entirely different than what they had lost,
then that is entirely up to them. These programs are very restrictive,
though, offering only help during a transition, rather than help to pursue
opportunity.

The result is that none of these programs do anything to truly stimulate
economic growth and development through innovation. They help to
sustain consumption by assisting in the matching process between employer
and employee, but this ignores the vast majority of what is required for a
labor force to be mobile in the manner necessary to achieve market efficiency. None of these programs do no, in any way, resemble a structure
necessary to facilitate the pursuit of freedom. None of these programs
account for the full dynamics of an evolving economy that requires continuous innovation, which must allow companies that cannot efficiently compete in the market (including labor markets) to dissolve, so that more
innovative companies that contribute to the continued progress of the
nation might thrive. Facilitating the pursuit of freedom through labor
mobility in a dynamic economy requires a greater degree of flexibility in
function, so that the market can best decide how to utilize the resources
allocated to the pursuit in question. In other words, such a program must
facilitate the pursuit of goals and passions which drive economic growth and
development—not just try to maintain the status quo through matching
programs.

In the *Wealth of Nations*, Book 1, Chapter 8, Paragraph 17, Adam Smith states:

> When in any country the demand for those who live by wages, laborers, journeymen, servants of every kind, is continually increasing; when every year furnishes employment for a greater number than had been employed the year before, the workmen have no occasion to combine in order to raise their wages. The scarcity of hands occasions a competition among masters, who bid against one another, in order to get workmen, and thus voluntarily break through the natural combination of masters not to raise wages.

That is the manner in which a grant program will perpetuate the pursuit of freedom. By facilitating people in the pursuit of their passions (the logistics of which are discussed in detail in Chap. 9), there will be a large increase in the volume and variety of employers, more evenly distributed across the geography. The increased competition for workers will not only increase real wages, but there will be demand for a wider variety of skill sets than currently possibly in the current era of automation and mass production. Thus, people will have the freedom to move geographically if they need to or if they want to, because there will be a wider array of employers. People will be have greater freedom to switch companies if they want, or to switch jobs if they are able. They will have greater freedom to negotiate in labor markets, increasing their wages, and improving working conditions such as the work/life balance. These improved wages and conditions will afford more people the opportunity to pursue the acquisition of new skills and education so that they can break free of the professional "rut" in which so many people find themselves after years doing the same thing. By creating a structure that allows the everyday genius with an innovative new plan to break free from wage slavery, that freedom will spread to others, and as people pursue their newfound freedom, it will create a more efficient economy that has a labor force that is not only highly mobile, but highly responsive to the evolution in market forces. This type of stimulus is critical to the health of a nation, and the continued advancement of humanity. As stated in a 2013 report from the Bureau of Labor Statistics (BLS), "With the persistent high levels of long-term unemployment, a concern exists that individuals' skills will deteriorate or the individuals will become permanently discouraged from job seeking. High unemployment likely inhibited the usual churn that helps create better matches between worker skills and employer needs, hurting economic efficiency."

P.S.: There is yet another freedom that is critical to the health of the economy, but which will only make sense within the context of this chapter and beyond. So keep this thought in your mind, for now, that the freedom of communication is vital. The distribution of information and knowledge between people is the primary stimulus of new ideas and innovations which allow humanity to advance. Any limits on communication, expression, the press, speech, or any other form in which information and knowledge is passed can function only to limit innovation.

PROFILE: RODERICK WHITTLE

Roderick has been working on cars for his entire life. Even before he could legally get a formal job, while other kids mowed lawns or babysat children, Roderick would do simple car maintenance for people to earn money. As he got older, and learned more, the jobs he did for people became more complicated until he was working full-time, self-employed as a mechanic, even going as far as to pass the exams necessary to become certified as a master mechanic. In order to make sure he was doing everything within regulation, he moved his operations to an industrial district. The district, a large, unlabeled space on the service drive of a major freeway in the suburbs, included row after row of buildings, each partitioned into several empty suites. Keep driving all the way to the back row, and on the opposite side of the building, toward the middle, you would find Roderick's shop: The Car Whisperers. He already had a small but consistent client base which he could expand through networking, so it was not a problem that his shop was nearly impossible to find, or that legally he could not put a sign at the side of the road to let people know where he was located. It did not matter, anyway, because this was just a transitionary location where he would operate until he could execute the real plan.

Roderick had something of a revolutionary new idea for the industry. At least, it was something that was not currently available in the area, so he intended to introduce a brand new type of mechanic service to the market and gain a competitive edge through his innovative new approach. He intended to offer a mobile mechanic service—one that did not necessarily require a stationary location at all—but one which would have the freedom to travel to wherever the customer was located (or at least where their car was located) and perform the work there. Roderick was confident in his analysis of the market—this would be more convenient and faster for the customers, and it would be cheaper to operate so that he could charge less than traditional auto mechanics. He was certain that this operating model was more efficient than the traditional one, ensuring that his plan succeed.

More to the point, it was necessary that this plan succeed. By the time he developed this idea in full, he had been working on cars for so long that he felt broken. His body was "worn down and beat-up", making the work difficult for him to perform. Each day was a struggle, and he hated it. He hired people temporarily during those times he needed a bit of extra help, and knew it was time to hire those people permanently so operate the mobile service so that he could use his time and knowledge in a manner that maximized his contributions: by operating the business and shaping it to watch his visions become reality. He would hire a total of six people full-time, and two part-time, and keep non-income operating costs between $3000 and $5000 per month, depending on volume.

He never did achieve the freedom to realize that dream, though. Regulations forced him to put his operations in a formal shop thereby increasing his overhead costs. Regulations forced him to take loans to go through a formal training process to learn what he already knew to get his master mechanic certification—loans which was not required to repay. Regulations prevented him from properly advertising the only location he could afford. He never did make enough money to afford a better location, and he never did save enough money to afford the start-up costs of his mobile business. It would have taken Roderick $50,000 to get his start-up running. Since his operating costs consisted 90% of labor, and he could charge by the job, that was not much of a concern, nor was equipment since he already owned the majority of what would be required. Still, even self-employed, a combination of circumstance and regulation put him in a position of self-imposed debt slavery. Working 70 hours per week and earning roughly $500 per week in income, he was making less than minimum wage. He hated working on vehicles but had a passion for entrepreneurship, and was willing to do it so long as he was free to pursue his final goal. Realizing that this goal was not going to be achieved, The Car Whisperers closed their doors forever.

Today, Roderick is a managing mechanic for a school district, in charge of the operations that keep the busses running. This is exactly what he was trying to prevent. He is now physically struggling every day to work on even larger vehicles, in a position with no potential for innovation or entrepreneurial spirit, controlled closely by regulations at every level. His story does not end in tragedy, though. No, it is at this point that Roderick experiences first-hand many of the things which will be described in the second half of the book. Without even realizing it, Roderick became a living example of those things which make the economy grow.

Roderick got married. While this would normally be completely irrelevant, he got married to someone who had a particular set of knowledge, and when they exchanged knowledge they came up with a new innovation they could pursue together. With the dissolution of The Car Whisperers (something which will be referred to in the second half of this book as "creative destruction"), the resources and labor were made available to pursue this new venture. Despite hating his job with the school district, his income was high enough that it has allowed them to save enough to pay for the start-up costs of their new idea, and give them the freedom to survive during the start-up phase so that they are not forced to try and manage a start-up while working full-time simply for the sake of earning an income.

What is this new idea? At its core, their new venture is to help people pursue their own freedom. Through a unique approach to non-profit community centers that raises their own revenues, they will be giving people the skills and experience that are required to remain mobile within the labor force, and to pursue a life free of the restraints placed upon them by the systemic poverty described by Adam Smith, and all the terrible things that are associated with it. They are working to create economic development—the improvement of the quality of life for people in an area which desperately needs it—and they are doing it in a manner which also contributes to the economic growth of that area, and the improved efficiency and competitiveness of the labor force, creating a better nation.

BIBLIOGRAPHY

Smith, A. (1817). *An inquiry into the nature and causes of the wealth of nations.* Edinburgh: Printed for S. Doig and A. Stirling.

Taillard, M., & Giscoppa, H. (2013). *Psychology and modern warfare: Idea management in conflict and competition.* New York: Palgrave Macmillan.

U. S. Census Bureau. (n.d.). *Historical income tables: Households.* Retrieved April 08, 2017, from https://www.census.gov/data/tables/time-series/demo/income-poverty/historical-income-households.html

CHAPTER 6

The Pursuit of Equality

Money cannot buy happiness, but it can resolve many of those things which cause us distress. It can eliminate the possibility of homelessness by paying-off a mortgage or other loans, it can ensure we have access to proper healthcare, it can allow us to feed our children, and much more. Financial trouble is the #1 cited reason for divorce in the United States, and for so many people, their ultimate financial goal is simply to be without any major threats to their health and relationships. Multiple studies have objectively proven this fact in recent years. A 2010 study by Deaton and Kahneman stated that a person in the United States must earn $75,000 per year to avoid the distress of financial threat. More recently, a 2016 study by Clingingsmith stated that as a person's income increases, their level of unhappiness decreased greatly up until the point they earn $80,000 per year (roughly the same conclusion as the 2010 study, once you consider inflation rates), and then happiness increases at a slower rate until a person begins earning $200,000 per year, at which point additional increases in income will have no effect on improving happiness. Of course these studies used national average, so you can adjust that income level slightly based on the cost of living in your area compared to the average, but at no place within the United States will the amount be very far from the annual income stated. So, for 98% of the nation, and a much larger percentage of the world, they will never truly understand what it means to be without financial distress, though—at least, not under the current system.

© The Author(s) 2017
M. Taillard, *Aspirational Revolution*,
DOI 10.1007/978-3-319-61771-8_6

There is a quick equation we can use to illustrate happiness:

$$\text{Happiness} = \frac{\text{Reality}}{\text{Expectations}}$$

In other words, if your expectations of what you should experience are higher than the reality of what you experience, this will reduce happiness. On the other hand, if you get more than you expected, then that increases happiness. There are a variety of studies in marketing that help to validate this, at least in terms of consumer behavior, but whether or not it functions as a long-term generalization is debated. What we can say for certain, though, is that people expect that they should be able to live without the Sword of Damocles hanging over their heads at all times—they expect that they should be secure in the knowledge that they are not at serious risk of losing their most basic needs—yet because of the current economic paradigm, the financial distress that people feel is quite real. People expect that if they work hard that they will be able to eliminate this financial distress, and yet the reality for 98% of the national population is much lower, causing unhappiness, and even desperation. You might recognize the use of Expectations as a variable from the discussion on Temporal Motivational Theory in Chap. 3, wherein the degree to which a person expects to gain value increases their degree of motivation. This has vast implications for overall human progress, so understanding this cause and the resolution is critical to continued economic growth and development.

It is not actually a single thing that causes the socioeconomic disparity to grow, preventing the majority of people from achieving financial stability, but rather a collection of related things which, together, form a singular process. For lack of a formal name for this process—one which prevents the free market from functioning properly—I have come to call this market failure National Income Misallocation. Quite simply, within the free market, national income naturally agglomerates into increasingly vast concentrations until the national economy stops functioning entirely. It is a very real phenomenon which occurs in every nation around the world, and throughout history. Since the end of World War II, the United States began with a 20-to-1 difference in income between the wealthy and that earned by the average American (meaning the difference between the top 2% of earners and the remaining 98%). By 1980, this more than doubled to a 42-to-1 ratio, then in the year 2000 this jumped to 120-to-1, and finally in 2013 the available data ends with a massive difference in income of 354-to-1.

This is a process which occurs naturally, and there are examples in many nations throughout history, ancient and modern. That is not to say it is a good thing; quite to the contrary this eventually results in economic devastation, which is why it is considered a market failure. It is not even that the wealthy are so very rich that is the problem, but rather the problem arises as a result of the majority of the population losing their share of total national income over time. In the United States, although real wages (wages adjusted for inflation) for 98% of the population have remained constant since the 1940s, during that time the top 2% of earners experienced more than 100% of the total average wage growth. In other words, if the total amount of income growth in the United States is equal to 100%, then the very rich have earned more than 100% of that income growth because the majority of people experienced a loss of their total share of income. So, as the economy grows, and income remains stagnant, it means that only 2% of the nation is actually benefitting from the increased rates of production and efficiency. The growth socioeconomic disparity is not under debate—the data is easily confirmed using any of a variety of government sources, such as the Internal Revenue Service (IRS), Congressional Budget Office, and others (Fig. 6.1).

This problem stems from differences in something known as MPC, which is the percentage of your income you spend. People at the highest

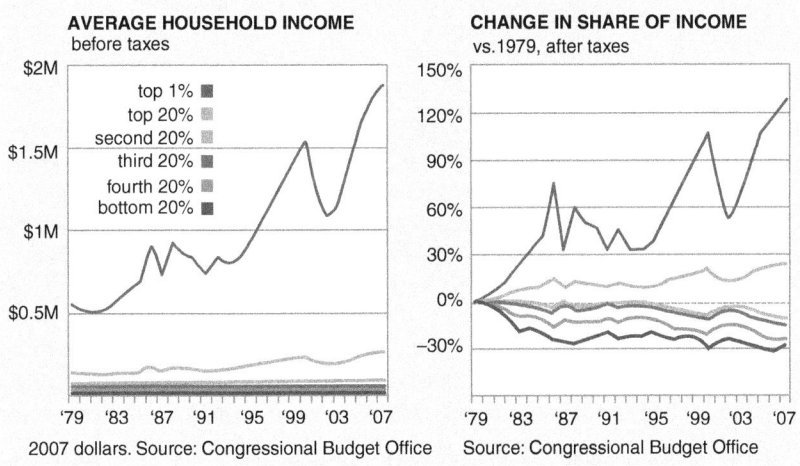

Fig. 6.1 Income inequality

levels of income spend roughly 20% of their total earnings, giving them an MPC of 0.2. The majority of the nation has an MPC between 0.9 and 1.0; living paycheck-to-paycheck. The remaining proportion of your total income is your MPS, marginal propensity to save. Ideally, this money is invested—even if an individual puts it in the bank, the bank then invests it in the form of loans. This is not entirely true, though. Ignoring the money that is held in overseas tax shelters, even when the money is put into a bank account, a percentage of that money will be held as a result of fractional reserve ratios (banks need to keep a percentage of all deposits on-hand to manage the daily goings-on of operating a bank). As for the money which is loaned by banks, whether it does anything to create economic growth and development is a matter which will be discussed in this chapter and Chap. 7, but for now suffice it to say that it does not to provide opportunities for people to find financial security.

It is the difference in MPC which drives the systematic failure of the growing wealth disparity. When you have lots of money, you do not need to borrow money for consumption such as car loans, student loans, or even necessarily for mortgages. For those times that the wealthy do borrow money, they are considered a very low credit risk given their high income, and so they are charged a lower interest rate. Thus, purchases of an equivalent nature between someone who is wealthy and someone who is not will result in significant differences in prices paid. In other words, not only does earning more money help make you rich, but being rich makes everything cheaper, all contributing to a much lower MPC. This low MPC has vast implications, starting with the investing opportunities made possible with the money that is not spent.

In order to make money by investing, first you need money to invest, but once you do, you can do something very important: diversify your income streams. According to the Urban-Brookings Tax Policy Center, the very rich only make about 35% of their total income from their wages, the remaining money comes from investments, self-employment such as through consulting, business ownership, inheritances and through marriage, and so forth.

Most investments are made in businesses, and many of these investments are in technological innovations which replace labor with capital. This increases efficiency but puts the nation in a position where not everyone needs to work in order to meet demand, thereby increasing the negotiating power for these businesses to demand labor at lower wages, and cutting costs to increase return on investment. As a wealthy investor, then, rather than simply working for your money, you are making more money simply because you already had money. This means you have multiple sources of income.

When you diversify your income streams, you are not reliant on any single employer, and that gives you a better negotiating position in the labor markets. You have the freedom to say, "No, I can afford to keep looking for a better offer." Having this ability presents the image of success, increasing demand for your labor regardless of whether or not you are any good at your job. According to The Economist Intelligence Unit, using data showing that between 2000 and 2010 total executive earnings increased over 110%, corporate performance actually decreased by several measures—better pay for doing a worse job. If executive performance is poor despite increasing levels of automation, then economic growth must inherently come from the employers during that period, and their income actually decreased as a ratio of total economic growth. We will get to that later in this chapter, though.

Investments can take a wide variety of forms. Besides stocks, and bonds, and venture capital, having large amounts of money also allows you to invest in methods of changing government policy, and public opinion in a manner that proactively creates an environment which is favorable for you. Industries, companies, and even individual people hire lobbyists to convince government officials to take a particular course of action that will generate income for the investor—the amount of money they make by changing government policy is much more than the cost of hiring the lobbyist. Investors will also contribute heavily to political campaigns, which either gets candidates elected who already support your policies, or entice politicians to support those policies in order to garner campaign funding. The latter of these is accomplished because candidates know money wins elections, and by accepting that campaign funding the politician now must be a good steward to their donors and support their policies. You can also donate directly to the political parties themselves, or to political action committees, which then also have significant influence on the funding and support of individual campaigns and the official stance of major political parties. Besides hard and soft campaign contributions, it is also possible to offer cushy, high-paying jobs to elected officials by putting them on the board of directors, or in executive management, or as a private consultant. Elected officials, not being subject to the same laws as the general public, can accept gifts, participate in insider trading, and any number of other activities which create a conflict of interest between policy-making and personal financial gain that would land a typical government employee in prison.

Having money buys much more than just government policy: it buys public opinion. Through advances in social psychology, public relations, and marketing, we have become very good at engineering what a population believes. The first formally written method of accomplishing this, called the Mohawk Valley Formula, was created to turn public opinion against labor unions back in the early twentieth century; and methods have only become more sophisticated. On this matter, though, I would refer you to the book *Psychology and Modern Warfare*, published by Palgrave Macmillan.

In other words, money is power and it is used to make more money through a wide variety of investments. This is then passed-down to the younger generation as an inheritance, wherein the children of those with money can simply hire someone to manage their wealth, so that they not only do not have to actually perform any work themselves, but they do not even necessarily need to know how to manage their own money. The Walton family, who owns Wal-Mart, have Forbes "Self-Made Score" ratings as low as possible, meaning they did nothing to earn a dime of what they own—have done nothing to contribute to the economic growth and development which fuels their wealth. The intergenerational passing of accumulated wealth functions as a seed for the next generation of growing inequality.

This is all a stark contrast to the vast majority of the nation, for whom survival necessities like housing, food, utilities, and so on compose over 99% of their total income. A portion of that money which is spent immediately goes into someone's pocket. Coming back to the Walton family, they are among the wealthiest individuals on the planet, earning their wealth from people who are spending all their money buying necessities like food and clothing. Much of that money goes to hire employees and stimulate production of the things which are being purchased, that is true, but the cash flows are consistently flowing in an upward direction, which is supported quite clearly in the data provided earlier in this chapter.

For the majority of people, taking loans to afford a car, house, education, and so forth, requires paying much more for these things than their actual value. This is because they must rely more frequently on loans, and the interest rates on those loans tend to be much higher. Since there is no money to invest remaining after paying the bills, a person becomes dependent entirely on their wages, rather than being able to generate more income and diversifying their income streams. Being dependent on a single source of income, that leaves people completely at the mercy of the employers, who are known as "price-makers" in the labor markets—they set the wages—while people will take any work that becomes available simply because they are desperate, even if that work is only part-time, pays far less than a standard living wage, or includes terrible working conditions.

With crushing debt and low wages, people end up paying a high percentage of everything they make as interest payments. Since loans are a form of investment for the lender, the interest payments being made are considered the return on investment. These interest payments represent a direct transfer of wealth from low-income to high-income individuals based simply on who already had money. This poverty is passed-down to future generations, too, and not just in the form of unpaid debt being transferred. It is proven that, although upward income mobility is not decreasing, it is still nearly impossible. Someone born to a low-income family has only about a 5% chance of moving into a higher socioeconomic state. Less access to quality education, less ability to socialize within networks of influential people, or be considered for high-income jobs keep low-income individuals in a position of low income. A person who does not have any money will rarely learn how to properly manage money—they will have no practice with such things as investing or capital management, so they will have no financial skills to teach their children.

The socioeconomic disparity also extends to the international community. There is a phenomenon known as the North-South Gap, wherein the vast majority of nations south of the equator tend to be poor, least developed nations, while the world's economic growth and development is almost exclusive to nations north of the equator. Globally, the line of what is considered poor is whether or not you are earning the equivalent of $1 per day in US currency. Even despite the differences in the cost of living in most nations, this forces a large percentage of the global population to survive on local barter systems and subsistence farming just to survive. Both intranational and international growth disparities result from the same mechanical failure in the free market: using the resources one already has available to them in order to earn more resources, then continuing to do so to the detriment of those who do not have resources. The wild animals in some regions, such as horses and oxen, could be domesticated far more easily than those of other regions, or the land more easily cultivated for farming, creating a difference in the ability of people to produce more than they needed and then trade the surplus for a profit. Whether a civilization made the transition to the Bronze Age depended entirely on whether they had ample stores of copper available to them. Over millennia, we find that some regions developed highly advanced civilizations, while others still failed to master early techniques such as farming. Many of these nations turned to the developed nations seeking assistance in achieving similar levels of economic growth and development, only to find their resources being exploited to the benefit of others with little or no benefits being produced for themselves. Even today we find the mechanics that perpetuate the international differentials in economic development are in many ways identical to those which perpetuate the socioeconomic disparities within a single nation.

This is all expressed in terms of something called the Gini Coefficient, which is a calculation produced that measures the amount of financial inequality in a nation. A Gini Coefficient of 0 means that everyone is financially equal, while a G value of 1 means that only one person owns all the wealth. This is perhaps best illustrated using the Lorenz Curve (Fig. 6.2).

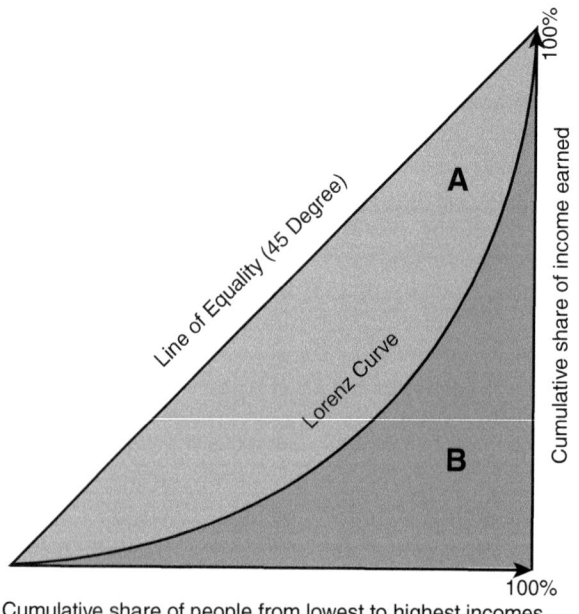

Fig. 6.2 Lorenz curve

Using the United States as an example of a single nation, the Central Intelligence Agency (CIA) estimates that the United States had a G value of 0.45 in 2007, which is the 43 most unequal nation in the world, slightly more equal than Cameroon but not quite as equal as Peru. The Organization for Economic Cooperation and Development is a little more forgiving, giving the United States a G value of 0.374 in 2007, but over time that has consistently worsened until the most recent data in 2014 in which the United States had a G value of 0.394; which is just slightly less equal than Turkey but a bit more equal than Mexico. As for the global disparity and the North-South Gap, this is far more pronounced. Using the most recent CIA data, the most financially equal nation is Slovenia (just south of Austria) with a G value of 0.237, while Lesotho (a small nation in the middle of the nation of South Africa) has a devastating G value of 0.632.

The solution to which we so often turn, as discussed in Chap. 2, is to provide services which help people maintain a minimum quality of life. There are those who support eliminating the disparity as a matter of human rights but their suggestions for fixing it treat only the symptoms rather than resolving the root cause, which will only be a temporary solution and have implications for trade, growth, inflation, and national debt. Those who are against attempting to treat the socioeconomic disparity have forgotten that even the wealth and success of the wealthy will be devastated if the disparity grows too large but, in some ways they have a point—the socioeconomic disparity is not the problem, it is merely a symptom of the real problem—national income misallocation. That is a problem which cannot be resolved by providing aid to the poor, but can only be fixed by addressing the underlying structural failure in the market by fundamentally changing the paradigm we use to stimulate economic growth, thereby preventing people from becoming poor in the first place.

For people to improve equality in socioeconomic status, there must be greater equality in labor market transactions. The concentration of capital which was discussed earlier in this chapter allows employers to function as monopsonies, which is the opposite of a monopoly. In other words, in a monopsony market, there is only one buyer in a market of many sellers. Although the labor market is not a true monopsony, the increasing concentration of capital which results in the increasing dominance of large companies, gives labor markets monopsony characteristics. The economic mechanism by which labor unions function was to decrease the number of competing suppliers of labor relative to the number of consumers of labor, thereby reducing or eliminating the role of employers as price-makers. Labor unions did accomplish their role for a limited time, but their failure to fix the underlying problem of national income misallocation eventually led to the erosion of their influence. Instead, the matter must be resolved by creating a structure in which competition and creativity can thrive. This requires people to focus on increasing the number of new-entrants via entrepreneurship and self-employment to increase the amount of free market competition not only in labor markets but in the markets for goods, and increasing the number of people pursuing their ideas for research and invention to disrupt existing markets. It requires people to pursue their passions, as described in Chap. 3.

Clearly not everyone will be so inclined to pursue some new venture. Probably most people are happy to find a consistent job that offers decent wages, preferably working with people whose company they enjoy. As previously discussed in this chapter, though, opportunities such as that are eroding—wages no longer pay for the cost of living, benefits such as medical insurance are all but completely extinct, and as the quality of the labor markets declines, the amount of friction between employers and workers increases. In fact, as competition for jobs increases, shortages of work even increases friction in society-at-large as people look at each other as a threat to their own financial well-being. Particularly during times of high unemployment, nations often seek a scapegoat, such as "the immigrant" who steals jobs, or "the foreigner" overseas to whom we send jobs, or generally some other minority group. While clearly this is the result of a more natural process rather than the fault of some convenient political scapegoat, knowing that is of little consolation to those who are struggling, which includes the majority of everyone.

As with all things in this book, however, the solution is derived directly from the things which cause the problem. The labor markets, once driven by those seeking passion and purpose, will undergo a transformation. It will increase the volume and variety of employers competing for workers.

PROFILE: TONY MATTA

TMFM, it stands for "Tony Makin' Food Matta". One might be excused for misunderstanding, because it is an odd acronym to call one's self, but if you spend more than just a few minutes with Tony it all becomes clear. Tony works alongside celebrity chef Wolfgang Puck, helping manage

Puck's restaurant at the MGM Casino in Detroit as a specialty sous chef. It is one of those rare places where the food truly is exquisite, as should be expected from a chef such as Puck, who has catered to the jet setters of the world. Tony's cooking does more than capably represent the type of haute cuisine that warrants a meal priced in the triple digits, though, because it provides a unique perspective unlike anything available even from Puck, himself. Although Tony clearly cherishes his role at the MGM, he does not deny that his personal background makes him yearn to provide something different—something that will generate greater value than even he realizes.

Tony says that although "selling a steak for $150 is cool and all, I would rather sell someone a nice meal for $30". For him, his cooking is not only his job in which he provides a valuable product to consumers, but it is an art form of a very unique nature. From the food, to the décor; from the front door to the kitchen; "the restaurant as a whole, including the guests, is all one big organism that changes every day. Every day you start with a new canvas, and a new experience." He knows he can make that artistic experience available to a broader population, giving people the opportunity to enjoy it at a price range that is more accessible. This is the population he knows, because this is the population he belongs to and from which he has his roots.

Years ago, in his eyes, there was no opportunity. He had worked in restaurants since he was 13 but was not aware there was any potential—any hope for a future. Falling into despair, he turned to short-term solutions in alcohol and narcotics to help him cope. He credits his brother with enrolling him in the culinary arts program at Schoolcraft College. It is an unassuming community college in the Detroit suburbs, so for many, including Tony, it did not seem to present any real opportunity to change things. It was not until he began that he became aware that hidden deep within the campus is one of the nation's top programs for culinary arts. Suddenly, he found direction. Suddenly, his life began to make sense, as he discovered a path to a future in which he could make a decent living doing something that brought him a creative outlet. Suddenly, it no longer made sense to spend his time getting high to cope with life, because life now had a purpose to pursue.

Prior to MGM, the best opportunity he was offered was a job earning $30,000 per year. Even today, after years of training, and then working to run a world-class restaurant for the last three years, Tony makes $54,000 per year. That is $10,000 more than when he first started at MGM, but this still falls well short of the benchmark $80,000 per year required to achieve true opportunity for financial equality, as shown in the studies described at the beginning of this chapter. Tony has met his physiological, safety, and esteem needs—even reaching into self-actualization—but with student loans to repay and the desire to start a family, he was very blunt when he says that the biggest impediment to him starting something revolutionary was "money".

The truly important part, though, is that this impediment is preventing a very important impact on economic growth and development. Tony, this single individual, if afforded the opportunity to pursue his passion in-full, would create roughly 20 new just at his restaurant: "2 floor managers, 1 head bartender, 3 bar tenders, 5 servers, 2 bar backs, 5 cooks, 2 dishwashers, and me". Ignoring the economic stimulus effects of increasing monetary velocity, by simply facilitating the aspirations of a single individual, there was an increase in competition for labor equivalent to 20 new jobs. That would then grow even more, as he expanded operations, potentially even opening multiple locations. Even more importantly, he intends to use his restaurant as a teaching kitchen, wherein he can train others to follow the same path he did, perhaps even avoiding the pitfalls of accumulating student loans. The result would multiply the stimulus over time, not only by increasing the number of people driven to find their passions, but through the passing of knowledge to a new generation, with their own new ideas, developing innovations that drive progress (the matters of information spillover and innovation will be discussed in detail in Chap. 9).

Based on the finances of the restaurants he has managed in the past, he estimates that the cost of opening his own vision would be a mere $200,000; prudently using used or refurbished equipment for much of his needs. He projects that the restaurant would break-even in three years. A successful business that operates indefinitely for years, immediately creating 20 new jobs and expanding that number over time, all of which is generating new tax revenues without any increase in the tax rates. A natural stimulus mechanism called the multiplier effect (which will be discussed further in Chap. 10) will cause the initial growth to extend into secondary and tertiary transactions, and Tony's aspiration becomes not only an innovative new business, but a fiscally conservative contribution to improving labor markets, thereby helping to increase economic growth and improved quality of life. How many people are there like Tony? Their collective impact on decreasing the socioeconomic gap via free market forces would do much in assuring people they can achieve that benchmark level of

income required to remove financial distress without the need for expensive
and inefficient social support programs.

BIBLIOGRAPHY

Belsie, L. (n.d.). *The causes of rising income inequality*. Retrieved April 08, 2017,
from http://www.nber.org/digest/dec08/w13982.html

Bloomquist, K. (2003). *Tax evasion, income inequality and opportunity costs of
compliance*. Washington, DC: IRS.

Clingingsmith, D. (2016). Negative emotions, income, and welfare: Causal estimates from the PSID. *Journal of Economic Behavior & Organization, 130*, 1–19.
doi:10.1016/j.jebo.2016.07.004

Country Comparison :: Distribution of Family Income – Gini Index. (n.d.).
Retrieved April 08, 2017, from https://www.cia.gov/library/publications/the
-world-factbook/rankorder/2172rank.html

Dabla-Norris, E., Kochhar, K., Suphaphiphat, N., Ricka, F., & Tsounta, E. (n.d.).
Causes and consequences of income inequality: A global perspective. Washington,
DC: International Monetary Fund.

Harris, E., & Sammartino, F. (2011). *Trends in the distribution of household income
between 1979 and 2007*. Washington, DC: Congress of the United States, Congressional Budget Office.

Kahneman, D., & Deaton, A. (2010). High income improves evaluation of life but
not emotional well-being. *Proceedings of the National Academy of Sciences, 107*
(38), 16489–16493. doi:10.1073/pnas.1011492107

Social and welfare issues, OECD Income Distribution Database (IDD): Gini,
poverty, income, Methods and Concepts. (n.d.). Retrieved April 08, 2017,
from http://www.oecd.org/social/income-distribution-database.htm

Stone, C., Trisi, D., Sherman, A., & Horton, E. (2017, April 07). *A guide to statistics on
historical trends in income inequality*. Retrieved April 08, 2017, from http://www.
cbpp.org/research/poverty-and-inequality/a-guide-to-statistics-on-historical-trends-
in-income-inequality

Taillard, M. (2013). *101 things everyone needs to know about the global economy: The
guide to understanding international finance, world markets, and how they can
affect your financial future*. Avon: Adams Media.

Taillard, M., & Giscoppa, H. (2013). *Psychology and modern warfare: Idea management in conflict and competition*. New York: Palgrave Macmillan.

PART 2

Understand

Now it is time to get to the point. So far we have explored those things which drive us, as individuals and as a society, to contribute our efforts through valuable production. We have explored the contradiction which exists for humanity in today's society as people struggle between their instinctual need for survival, and their instinctual need to pursue that which has assured the survival of the species. That which has brought our civilization to be so advanced, compared to our terrestrial competitors, though, now appears to be failing us—or perhaps we are failing to use it—but in either case something is causing the advancement of humanity to slow, and the solution has already been revealed in the first half of this book. Revealed, that is, in a somewhat indirect manner through descriptions of human pursuits, both in abstract and tangible ways.

In this second half of the book, entitled "Understand", we leave behind the stories and personal engagement. This portion of the book is entirely focused on the application of economic principles to objective data, and the analysis of economic modeling. All this is used to come to logical conclusions about the problem at hand and how to resolve it—the proposed economic methods contained within this half of the book, you will find, are nothing more than the natural extensions of the relevant fact. Perhaps it is a unique combination of ideas being utilized, or simply a unique perspective on those ideas which has inspired new solutions to the existing problems, but even though the proposed methods are entirely unique to this book, they exist wholly within the realm of very basic economic theory.

In truth, this was all inspired from my critical assessments of the idea of universal basic income (UBI) some years ago, at which point I was able to determine its failings. With the growth in popularity of the idea, though, came the need to look more deeply at it. The problems with universal basic income remained, but with a closer look it became clear what a proper solution would require. The only question became one of logistics, which was a simple enough matter, given that similar systems are already used for other purposes.

So, that is the point of "Understand": To explain the mechanics which caused us to thrive, the failings which now threaten that state, and to propose a brand new economic dynamic which will function as a resolution. As always, the basics are included, and the more advanced matters are written as simply as possible.

Once again, as with Part 1, for the sake of simplifying the process of using this book as a reference tool, here are some brief summaries of the chapters in Part 2. It seems particularly relevant for the second half of this book to include this brief summary, since there will be a greater volume of technical concepts and terminology used, so having a reference point by which you might be able to recognize the context in which the thing you seek was placed might prove to be quite useful.

Chapter 7: Past Potential

Within this chapter there is a detailed, though rather specialized, history of humanity. Beginning from the very beginning of human existence, this chapter explores how just a few key discoveries have taken us from being cave-dwelling hunter-gatherers, to the modern era of automated digital intelligence. This chapter describes each of three eras in history as an economic epoch, in which the primary manner in which we pursued the resources required for survival was permanently altered, fundamentally changing what it means to be human. Singular discoveries rarely change the world in such a significant manner, but there are natural cycles which were triggered—chains of events which, once begun, expanded along a predictable path toward their inescapable conclusion, until replaced by the next major economic epoch. The principles of economic gravity compose a large portion of this chapter, describing the lifecycles of cities and civilizations, the spread of people and the evolution of culture, and those forces which truly define the borders and identities of people as compared to the arbitrary and artificial borders defined by politics. All this is merely the result of innovations which increased the amount of production per person which was possible in an era, and how that relates to the size of the population which can be sustained at that production level.

CHAPTER 8: PAST OUR PRIME

Global economic growth is slowing, not just as a cyclical recession, but as part of a new norm as a consequence of the upper limit of production potential that exists under the current economic epoch. This slowdown is at the forefront of conversations at CATO, the International Monetary Fund (IMF), US BLS, and many others, but none of them seem to be able to agree on the source or resolution. The reason is that they are still working under old assumptions of the previous structure, failing to recognize that we have reached our maximum potential and have already begun to shift toward something brand new. Capital-based growth can only continue for so long. You simply cannot continue to automate and industrialize and digitize work, without creating a structure which utilizes humans in another manner. To turn back to labor is neither appropriate, nor is it possible. The size of the population has grown the point that the decreased efficiency could not sustain it. Instead, we must look to what allowed us to accomplish our achievements thus far, and determine how to use that not only to fix the current problem of a slowing economy, but how to continuously use that as a source for what comes next.

CHAPTER 9: CRUX OF THE PROBLEM

This chapter is the climax of the book. It explains exactly what is causing the problem of slowed economic growth to occur, and why all efforts to solve the problem thus far have failed. In this chapter you will find simple modeling of basic economic growth, which use a common production function at their core. This chapter explains how these growth models have been the primary driver of increased economic production until recently, the way they have been incorporated into fiscal and monetary policy, and the reason they are now failing to function properly. The emerging idea of a universal basic income is also addressed in this chapter, as it is a natural extension of those current methods which are failing, thereby explaining why universal basic income will also fail to generate the desired, instead delaying the inevitable while perpetuating the negative side effects in the process.

CHAPTER 10: A PRIME OPPORTUNITY

This chapter is the resolution of the book—the finale. Within this chapter you will find a detailed explanation of the proposed economic paradigm. It includes not only a very plain explanation of what needs to be done, but also the underlying economic theory in endogenous Schumpeterian Growth that makes it function properly. Also within this chapter is a very detailed explanation of the decision-making process for resource allocations, and the ways in which corruption and abuse are prevented. This chapter also touches just briefly upon how this proposal is an improvement upon competing proposals for a new economic paradigm.

CHAPTER 11: FUTURE POTENTIAL

The future looks bright. It is a bubbling pot where small businesses and other new entrants continuously rise to compete in the free market, bringing new products and new methods with them, forcing existing companies to either evolve or dissolve. It is a place where discovery and invention drive improvements not only to our lives, but to businesses with improve efficiency, and to governments which will have new tools through which to cut spending while simultaneously reducing the national debt, without sacrificing those things which are necessary to function coherently. Growth and development distribute geographically evenly, bringing with them jobs and community revitalization to impoverished areas. Though no one can foresee what things may come, we know the methods which will be used to bring them, and it yields a hopeful vision of the future.

CHAPTER 7

Past Potential

Human existence is defined almost entirely by the methods we use to acquire the resources of our survival—food, water, shelter, and so forth. There have been two major discoveries in which the primary manner in which we pursued the resources required for survival was permanently altered, fundamentally changing what it means to be human. The limits of human advancement are bound to the economic paradigm of the time. There have so far been three major economic epochs in all of human history, and the nature of each defined what could be accomplished during their time by the people who lived in that era. It only takes one tiny little change—the right idea at the right time—to change the course of human history. Each new economic epoch was initiated by a tiny revelation discovered originally by some common persons whose names are lost to history, at just the right time, and it spread. It was not the grand pronouncements of new inventions or processes, such was the wont of people like Thomas Edison and Henry Ford—they merely found ways to profit from the inventions of these new epochs. The original inception of the ideas came from unknown people in the population—the everyday geniuses who simply understood their own job well enough to recognize opportunity. It is from those humble beginnings that human civilizations suddenly surface, seemingly overnight, through the processes put into motion by the laws of economic gravity. These are the processes which has brought the rise and fall of entire empires, which shapes the spread of culture and language, and which defines the very nature of what it means to be human.

© The Author(s) 2017
M. Taillard, *Aspirational Revolution*,
DOI 10.1007/978-3-319-61771-8_7

As for the first economic epoch, you can think of it as merely the era prior to civilizations. This is the hunter-gatherer period, which spans the entire era of human history prior to roughly 10,000 BCE. Of course, the further back we try to look in time, the harder it is to get a full picture of how things happened, but thankfully (at least for the purposes of this book), we can also look to tribal groups who live in this same manner even today, particularly in the most isolated areas of the world, most famously in South America and Southeast Asia. So, although we will be discussing pre-historic Africa, our knowledge of the economic activity of the time will be supplemented using directly observed facts of modern analogues.

It is during this time in history; nomadic migrations which followed the seasons as they pursued migrating animals for hunting, and the edible plants which thrived. They were subject to the ebb and tide of nature. The amount of production possible and, therefore, the size of the population which was sustainable, were limited to natural trends in the populations of those things which were hunted. Times of shortages were sometimes predictable, such as regions which experience drought or winter seasons, but for many there were factors not well understood that could decimate entire civilizations by eliminating the source of their production.

The Natufian peoples, who lived at least as early as 12,500 BCE in an area of NE Africa and SW Middle East region called The Levant, were a transitionary society helping to demonstrate the shift from hunter-gatherer to agricultural societies. At the end of the last Ice Age (known as the Quaternary Glaciation), long dry seasons in this region allowed annual plants to die, and drop dormant seeds, which then regrew during the wet seasons. People became dependent on the continuous gathering of grains in this manner, and were able to settle in a single location because of the abundance and consistent availability of these plants. A drop in temperature associated with climactic fluctuations of a warming planet in the post-Ice Age era triggered an extended period of drought in the region called the Younger Dryas Event, during which time the grain plants died and were dominated by inedible plants associated with desert regions. It is thought that this event is what finally inspired the invention of agriculture, as the Natufian people would clear out the inedible plants and bring seeds from other regions where they were more available, thereby creating the first garden. As of writing this, this period was the first known in which people systematically altered their environment to make it more favorable. Before this time, however, during the final Ice Age, people clearly could not farm, and so not only were people forced to continuously move, ensuring they followed the source of food available, but were also subject to being hunted, themselves, by predators also following the same migration patterns. The continued existence of entire cultures around the world were at risk of failing as a result of resource shortages caused by things completely out of their control. Since the transition from hunting-gathering to farming occurred alongside the genesis of a sedentary lifestyle (i.e., one in which people live in a single region for long periods of time rather than continuously migrating), we will refer to the period prior to the invention of farming as the Nomadic Economic Epoch.

Note that the exact details on much of this are still vague. The exact dates and locations of events, the precise manner in which events occurred, are debated; but that is all a matter for the archaeologists. Much of the information we have about these eras are lost, simply being so old and ravaged by time that the remnants of these periods are eventually destroyed. Thankfully, for the purposes of this book, the things which we know for certain give us exactly what we need. We are not so worried whether the discovery of agriculture happened a century earlier and a few miles south of what we originally thought. This book, being an economics book, is more concerned with the process by which human civilizations developed, and so the best information currently available is more than sufficient for our purposes. With the advent of agriculture, though, record-keeping improved. In fact, one of the earliest written languages (perhaps the earliest), Cuneiform, was originally developed by the Sumerians in order to keep records of transactions and inventories. So, any period after the nomadic epoch will have much more detailed accounts with greater certainty.

With the realization that they could produce their own food rather simply collect it, it allowed people for the first time to stop their nomadic migrations and settle in a single location. It allowed them, for the very first time, to produce more resources than they needed. That is to say, for the first time, an average person could produce more food than they could eat, and give the remainder away to someone else. Not surprisingly, this concept became wildly popular. The idea that a single person could produce enough food to sustain an entire group of people was a real turning point for people who were good at growing food because then they could give the extra food to other people and then those people would do things in exchange for the food. So popular and fundamentally different was this idea that it changed the entire nature of human existence through the Agricultural Revolution, and humanity entered the second of its three economic epochs: The Agricultural Epoch.

Agriculture changed everything. This moment in history is important because it marks the start of economic growth. For the first time in history, a single person could start producing enough subsistence goods to sustain larger volumes of people. Even when you look at tribal hunter-gatherer cultures in the modern era, although they are working together they spend all their time, energy, and resources in the pursuit of subsistence. With the advent of farming came the luxury of surplus production, so that those who were not farming could spend their time in a manner in which new skills could be learned. More than that, this meant that one person could focus on producing food, sustaining several others with the output of their efforts in exchange for goods and services in which other people would specialize. Together, they can produce more total production than they could working on their own and generate gains from trade—economic growth which expanded at a rate faster than mere population growth. Consider Table 7.1 below.

Both Pat and Chris must make both food and clothes. Chris, having more working experience, can produce more total stuff than Pat, in the example. That means Chris has an absolute advantage, but notice that they are not as efficient at producing clothes as Pat. We know this because of the ratio of food to clothes production. In order to make 1 additional unit of clothes, Chris must give up 1.5 units of food. In contrast, in order to make 1 additional unit of clothes, Pat only needs to give up 0.5 units of food. Instead, Chris has a comparative advantage in food. By giving up 2 units of clothes, Chris can produce 3 units of food. So, Pat and Chris see this and decide to specialize and trade, as shown in Table 7.2.

Table 7.1 Production without trade

W/out trade	Food	Clothes
Pat	5	10
Chris	15	10
Total	20	20

Table 7.2 Production with trade

W/trade	Beer	Pizza
Pat	0	20
Chris	30	0
Total	30	20

By trading on their relative comparative advantages, they can produce more together than they could on their own, generating more collective wealth between them.

This is known as the division of labor and specialization. As each person focuses on a particular type of work, they become very good at it and increase the amount of production efficiency so that they can produce far more than if they tried to produce everything on their own. In other words, as everyone works at only the things in which they excel, not only will each person be able to improve their skills thereby becoming more efficient, but no person will waste vast amounts of their time trying to do something that someone else could do easily. There are still a minimum number of things that need to be accomplished for a community to survive, so in a very small community each person still needs to have a diverse set of skills, but they can still generate economic growth by using their collective efforts more efficiently. Individuals trading like this is something which has occurred since the dawn of humanity, though, as small communities of people relied on the separation of labor just to survive the harsh existence of their time. With the advent of agriculture, things changed.

Whatever it is a particular person or company is good at producing, or the function they are good at performing, is considered their competitive advantage. They consume fewer resources to perform that function, which means they are incurring fewer costs, and since they are producing market value with their labor, people are willing to buy their stuff for a price higher than the costs incurred, generating profit. When we look at what all the people in a community or civilization—when you aggregate the competitive advantages of everyone in a single economic body—the trends in their respective competitive advantages can be compared, and so it is called the comparative advantage. The functions of trade and transactions remain the same, but the measurement is shifted from the individual to the community. Through agriculture, fewer people could sustain an entire community, and so people can specialize in ever-narrowing skill sets, generating increasing growth rates.

With increased growth, the ability of that community to attract more trade increases, which is known as economic gravity, utilizing the equation of universal gravitation developed by Isaac Newton: $T = G((M_a M_b)/D_{ab})$. Though variations on this equation have proven somewhat more reliable, they all utilize this same equation at their core, which is actually the same equation used to calculate the gravitational pull of bodies in space. Simply put, it states that the amount of gravitational pull that something has is a function of the amount of mass, M, of the two bodies, and the distance, D, between them. G is the same gravitational constant utilized by Isaac Newton in his own equivalent equation of the Law of Universal Gravitation. For economic bodies, mass is measured typically in terms of Gross Domestic Product GDP (gross domestic product), while distance still refers to the geographic distance between them. So, what this means is that as the economic size of a community grows, more people from the surrounding area will travel there to try and sell their own goods, to purchase things they cannot get elsewhere, and to move there and specialize in their own particular skill. As the demand in the region grows beyond the capacity of individual people to supply, they will hire people to help, and people will begin moving to this region in order to find jobs and learn new skills. Producers of other goods will move closer to their suppliers and customers in order to cut the costs of production in what is known as economies of agglomeration. With farmers still keeping up with the growing population, a majority of people begin working in manufacturing.

At this point, the very nature of what it means to be human has changed on a global scale. Rather than pursuing subsistence on a small scale, survival now means learning a unique skill and using it as efficiently as possible in order to trade for the other things you need. Instead of a subsistence-based economy, the efforts of farmers now sustain entire civilizations which create things, forming a labor-based economy.

With greater numbers of manufactured goods, innovations in the types of tools being produced are made. Better tools are developed for the agricultural foundations upon which the civilization's economy is built, and new tools are being made to help increase production of those tools. Around 3300 BCE, someone discovers they can smelt copper and humanity enters the Bronze Age, and then around 1200 BCE it is discovered that iron can be forged and humanity enters the Iron Age, all of it expanding the diversity and volume of production, attracting greater volumes of people toward singular locations, forming cities.

The inventions and innovations developed during the Agricultural Epoch did help to stimulate improvements in the advancement of humanity, but in more incremental steps that expanded upon the revolutionary innovation of agriculture, itself. This is the difference between capital-based exogenous growth and knowledge-based endogenous growth that we'll discuss further in Chaps. 8 and 9. Investing in new tools and machinery requires people to learn how to use them helping to develop minor innovations that trigger greater degrees of growth within the parameters, since these incremental innovations tend to be variations on existing technologies which have their own upper limits on production potential. In terms of agriculture, although there were improvements in important tools such as the plow which made farming easier, it was still simply an incremental variation on farming, itself, and so when the Agricultural Epoch hit its upper limit there was no incremental innovation which could truly revolutionize human civilization in the same way that the innovation of agriculture did in the beginning. It took a brand new revolutionary innovation, which requires a direct emphasis on knowledge and innovation, rather than new tools.

Just as the gravity in space brings the mass of gas and dust together in greater volumes until it combusts into a star and starts producing energy, so too does economic gravity draw individuals toward a single location that creates economic energy in the form of production that pushes the city outwards. In order to accommodate the growing population, the city itself must grow either upward or outward, requiring the production of infrastructure. As the collective gains from trade between individuals in a single city create city surpluses, merchants were used along trade routes to facilitate exchanges between cities. There is also strong incentive to move resources and people out of the city. Cities, with all their people and production, tend to be crowded, noisy, and dirty; and all the infrastructure necessary to facilitate the larger population costs money, just as the increased demand for production allows for higher prices, increasing the cost of living within the city, itself. This gives strong incentive to move away from the city; producers looking to expand operations invest in lower-cost rural areas, those who can afford to move to areas with lower population density will do so in order to get away from the negative traits of urban areas, and when these things happen the tax dollars move away from the city with them. As a city expands outward, infrastructure costs increase, but once people and resources start moving out of the city, there is a decrease in the ability to pay for that infrastructure, and so begins the process of urban decay, exacerbating the problems associated with living and working in urban areas. Blight occurs as parts of a city become unusable, and crime starts to rise as a result of the psychological impact of seeing little or no future potential and a shortage of work, so the desperation for income and supplies results in people seeking alternative means when traditional jobs do not exist: selling drugs, shipping weapons, theft, and so on. These high rates of crime result in even faster destruction of property and overextends law enforcement, causing more people and investments to leave, and resulting in total dysfunction.

When stars consume all their mass, the energy they produce pushes their borders outward, and begins to shed layers until it eventually dies. Cities follow the same lifecycle if they are not managed properly, and to manage a city, that means balancing gravity and energy to create an equilibrium (Fig. 7.1).

In the early civilizations, the aristocracy would have multiple homes in the rural areas, so that when one became intolerably unhygienic, they would move to another one while the others are cleaned. This, of course, required the movement of people and resources to maintain the buildings and grounds, and the network of supporting laborers to produce food and clothing and everything else needed.

The Rapa Nui people of Easter Island, a vibrant civilization which no longer exists, is thought to have disappeared most likely as a result of such

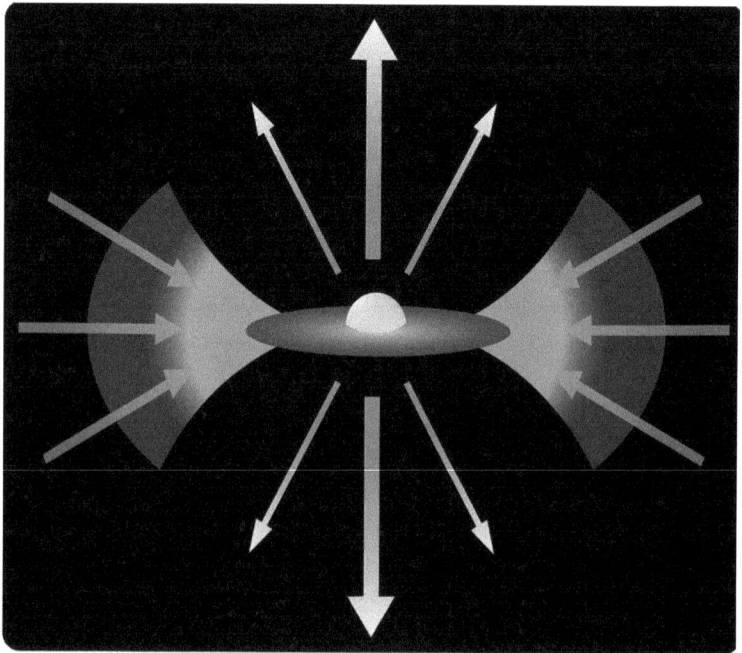

Fig. 7.1   Gravity and energy

factors. As the population of this agriculturally based civilization grew, the available resources could not sustain that population, resulting in either overconsumption or deforestation-induced famine (similar to the Dust Bowl in twentieth-century United States), and so the majority of the population disappeared (i.e., either they left the island, or starved, or something—it is not real clear). The Rapa Nui people still exist, with Census data showing that roughly 4000 people still identify as ethnically Rapa Nui, but the Easter Island-based civilization never recovered. The productive energy produced consumed all the economic matter available, and the Easter Island was not able to generate enough economic gravity to attract additional matter, so it was all dispersed except for a small remnant of what it once was.

When one star sheds its layers and dies, though, all that matter dispersed throughout space will often gravitate toward other nearby matter, becoming the seeds of new stars. The automotive manufacturing lost to Detroit as the city, as it once was, shed its layers and died, spread across the nation, as domestic and foreign auto manufacturers set up plants in rural parts of Indiana, Georgia, and other places. Over history, grand civilizations have risen and fallen, only to be replaced by new ones. The Romans still live in Rome, though the Roman Empire no longer exists as it once did, yet its fall gave rise to other great cities across the globe.

One of those great civilizations was Great Britain, wherein during the 1700s CE the people went through their own Age of Enlightenment (not to sound Eurocentric—other cultures have had their own periods of great intellectual contributions to the world, but this period in specific is relevant to the topic at hand). It was during this period that the production potential of a labor-based economy had reached its maximum, and the average amount of production per person was slowing. The cumulative advancements of humanity until that time culminated in the British Age of Enlightenment, during which many innovations were made in science and industry which allowed for production to be automated. That is to say, production, which was previously done by people, could be performed automatically by machine. The realization that steam or electricity or chemical reactions could be used to generate enough energy to create mechanical movements was as fundamentally significant to human advancement as the discovery of agriculture. The idea spread quickly, and inventions were developed with the intention to perform just about any task thinkable, both in the workplace and at home, and thus the Industrial Revolution brought forth the final and current economic epoch, the Automation Epoch.

What makes this epoch unique is the shift from a labor-based economy to a capital-based economy. It began, most significantly, with automated production of textiles, but quickly expanded from there. Machinery could accomplish tasks at speeds much more quickly than people, so the volume of production per person after the Industrial Revolution increased dramatically (Fig. 7.2).

The higher rate of resource production helped to sustain increased rates of population growth, but production has increased at a much greater rate, until recently when—for the first time in all of human history—the needs of the population could be met without full labor market participation. We will come back to that in a moment, though.

The Industrial Revolution is actually divided into two parts: the First Industrial Revolution and the Second Industrial Revolution (historians and economists are not generally known for being creative in naming things, though there is an elegant simplicity to the descriptive nature of these labels). The first was defined largely by the invention of steam power—or, that is to say, the invention of the method by which steam power could be

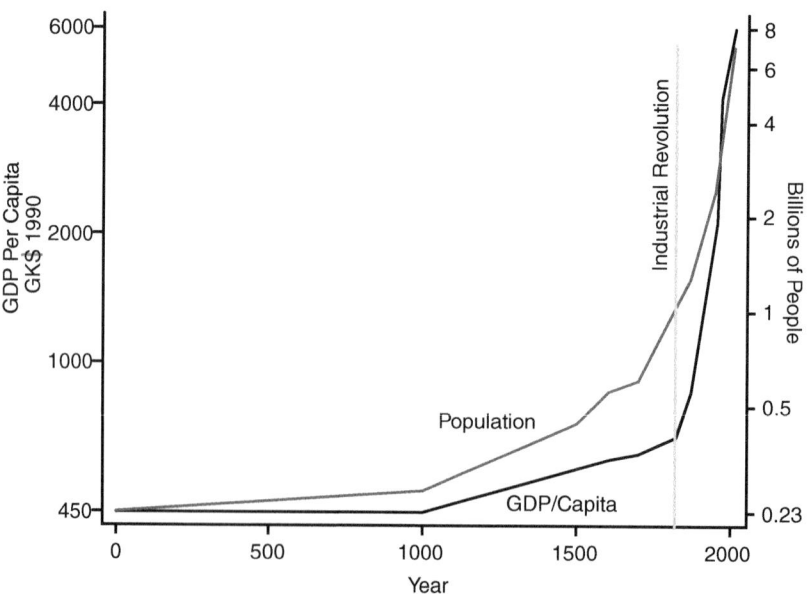

Fig. 7.2   Production and population growth (Source: The Maddison Project)

used practically. Previous designs could not produce enough power to function properly, or were not intended to function for the purpose of automation at all, but James Watt is credited with being the first to develop a method of harnessing steam in a way that could power pistons and create mechanical motion. This led to a huge array of incremental innovations based upon it, automating textiles, and toolmaking, and transportation. The second Industrial Revolution was really not marked by any particularly new revolutionary innovation. Advances based on the engine gave way to such things as the steam locomotive, steamboat, and so forth. Then as our understanding of the physics and chemistry of these things expanded, new methods of extracting energy became apparent. Rather than using coal, it was found that refining oil was more efficient, and even that electricity could be harnessed to power these automatic creations. The second Industrial Revolution is really marked more by a shift in geography from Britain, to the United States and Germany, both of whom dominated the automotive and steel industries. In the modern "digital age" of computers, the economic dynamic is still one of automating functions which already exist, without truly changing the dynamic of economic production. It still merely represents incremental shifts from labor to capital, rather than revolutionizing the manner in which resources are acquired.

The Automation Epoch began by replacing unskilled labor, as machines did tedious work that required repetitive motions without variation. This had little effect on employment because the unskilled laborers were then the ones to operate the machines. In other words, the machines were just better tools, allowing people to do their jobs more quickly. Economists were quick to theorize that this would always be the dynamic with technological progress, and they seemed to have a valid point. The advent of the assembly line in the United States incorporated people into the automation process. Each person had only one task to repeat constantly all day, but it was a task that required some degree of responsiveness, so that the machinery was used to facilitate the movement of work-in-process between people, when it was not doing the work, itself. Cities grew in size exponentially—massive populations congregated around industrial centers like Detroit, and financial centers like New York. The amount of economic gravity also grew, attracting people from all around the world, and when people were not attracted from afar, then the major industrialized nations were attracted to go afar by the massive economic potential in East Asia and went to forcefully open borders using something called "gunboat diplomacy", or used other forms of colonizing nations in other areas around the world which had yet to adopt industrial technologies. With the explosion of growth in economic energy and mass that came with mass production came predictable consequences. Vast wealth grew along isolated areas, such as the Gilded Age Mansions, while the cities became tremendously overpopulated and filled with squalor; diseases such as black lung and Cholera were rampant, while consumer product safety was at an all-time low, frequently causing fires, or illness from rotten food.

Once public health became a common concern, regulation largely remedied many of these issues, and that is where most stop thinking about industrialization, but it does go on. With advancements in robotics and computer engineering, automation has since replaced moderately skilled jobs; and thanks to more recent advances in artificial intelligence and data management, high-skilled jobs are also being automated. These things have made rates of production per person greater than anyone could have possibly imagined, which is both a blessing and a problem. We have vast resources with which to improve the quality of our lives and to solve problems, that is true, and we have access to extremely rapid modes of transportation and communication which allow for transactions around the world just as you would be making transactions the next town over, but we have failed to properly utilize it. Although matters of city sanitation are largely improved, the nature of the problems our production growth causes has expanded to cataclysmic levels, such as facing the challenge of global warming which we have caused. We have not actually solved the problems associated with growth, but rather expanded their scope.

We have also reached the limit of our potential growth and development in the Automation Epoch. Not only have we reached production potential that meets the needs of the population without everyone actively engaged in the labor force for the first time, but the number of people which are required in the labor force in shrinking. As we replace unskilled labor, then skilled labor, the diversity of jobs available shrinks, so that there is greater competition for jobs with skill sets still in need. As we continuously advance our technological progress, automation becomes cheaper and more efficient, so that fewer people can compete. In the 1700s we began our transition from a labor-based to a capital-based economy, and in the 2010s, we are nearer to a fully capital-based economy than we are a labor-based one.

In the Automation Epoch, this is what it means to be human: that the pursuit of survival is no longer about subsistence, and it is no longer about specialization of labor. In the Automation Epoch, survival means increasingly relying on innovation in order keep yourself relevant in the labor force—by using your ability to learn and reason in order to create or maintain capital. Clearly, there is a significant problem with that, though. Even in theory, under the current economic paradigm a divide has been gradually increasing that takes long-run aggregate supply (LRAS) and long-run aggregate demand (LRAD) out of a realistic equilibrium. Since LRAS is defined as the amount of production potential possible given enough time for the market to respond to changes in demand (in other words, the total production potential given current technological progress when used to its maximum potential), and that the current LRAS exceeds LRAD, production growth cannot be sustained. To say it another way, LRAS is defined by population and technology, establishing total possible production potential, but LRAD is defined almost exclusively by population, alone. As capital advances, the schism grows between the consumption that defines and sustains the economy, and the size of the population which can be sustained given the production potential of the available capital.

Things are slowing now. It is not just theory, either. As we will see in this chapter, the data conclusively demonstrates that there is a permanent slowing of global economic growth resulting, and though there is disagreement as to how to resolve the matter, there is clear to everyone that we have reached a plateau. It is time to accept the end of an era, and prepare to bring in a new era. If the current epoch is defined by our struggle to use learning and reasoning to remain relevant through the transition to a capital-based economy, then it stands to reason that the next epoch will be defined by our ability to learn and reason in order to advance that economy. This cannot be accomplished by using the same capital-based dynamics as the Automation Epoch, though—we cannot rely on capital to advance an economy already based upon capital. We need to discover what truly makes people unique—what has allowed us to thrive in ways no other species has been capable of—and maximize its potential.

BIBLIOGRAPHY

Diamond, J. (2017). *Guns, germs, and steel: The fates of human societies*. New York: W. W. Norton.

Harris, D. R. (2003). *The origins and spread of agriculture and pastoralism in Eurasia*. London: Routledge.

Taillard, M. (2013). *101 things everyone needs to know about the global economy: The guide to understanding international finance, world markets, and how they can affect your financial future*. Avon: Adams Media.

The Development of Agriculture. (n.d.). Retrieved April 08, 2017, from https://genographic.nationalgeographic.com/development-of-agriculture/

CHAPTER 8

Past Our Prime

National growth in the United States has slowed, and by all estimates it is expected to remain slow. Whereas GDP per capita has grown by an average of 2% per year since at least the mid-1800s despite dramatic changes in social, political, and economic conditions; it is now expected to slow to below at least 1.5% per year into the indefinite future. If that does not seem like a big deal, think about it like this: the production potential per person for the entire nation is projected to stay at least 25% lower than it has been since the Industrial Revolution. We have completely lost the gains in economic growth potential that we found in automation hundreds of years ago, and if you will recall from Chap. 6, a 25% drop in production growth means that the nation will not be able to sustain its current rate of population growth. A drop in resource growth must be accompanied by a drop in relative population growth, and if you consider for just a moment what it means that population growth must shrink and the manners by which such a thing will occur, then this prospect should terrify you. Already there are record numbers of people around the world who are displaced, seeking refuge in foreign lands simply to survive, while battle rages on in those regions most vulnerable to extreme resource scarcity.

The outlook for the global economy is no better, with slowing growth becoming an increasing problem at the forefront of the public's attention in China, Singapore, India, and across the entire EU region. The world as a whole, it seems, has not only struggled and failed to maintain its peak production potential, but that potential is dropping to levels which were attainable roughly near the beginning of industrialization, which means all

© The Author(s) 2017
M. Taillard, *Aspirational Revolution*,
DOI 10.1007/978-3-319-61771-8_8

the progress in resource production made possible through automation has been lost. Clearly the automation is not gone, though—machines and computers still dominate the landscape—so what has changed? Why is it that despite continuing incremental advancements in automation we appear to be losing the progress we have achieved? What could this loss mean to the global population and, most importantly, is there a chance we can prevent this fate?

This chapter began with some very bold, and rather grim, claims regarding the future of our global economy. It would be simple, and reasonable, for any rational person to discount them as the rantings of a lunatic preaching the end of days. Whether or not we are discussing the end of human civilization—the "end of days" scenario—depends on your time horizon. Eventually all things must end, but whether or not that will be realized in the more immediate future ("immediate" meaning within the next several generations, rather than the next several years) depends almost entirely on us. Whether or not I am a lunatic in making these claims is not up for debate, however, but in order to support the validity of the claims being made we need to dig into the data and pull out supporting citations. After all, why should you take my word for it, when the global economics community have all come to roughly the same conclusion, many of them with more dire predictions than those being estimated within these pages?

Estimates of the potential growth rate per capita, under optimal circumstances (which makes these estimates even more depressing), include:

Harvard University economist Dale Jorgenson: 1.05%
Northwestern University economist Robert Gordon: 1.58%
Federal Reserve Bank economist John Fernald: 1.36%
Congressional Budget Office: 1.55%

According to the CATO institute, this slowdown can be attributed to a perfect storm of factors. They cite such things as the fact that during the twentieth century women entered the workforce, and that we can only introduce that change once, but they fail to recognize that this was accounted for during the WWII economic boom, and that over the long-term trends, 2% growth was sustained well before women entered the workforce, and well after, so that this factor does not seem to have had an impact on the productivity per person—just the amount of total productivity given an increase in the total number of people. CATO also cites decreases in total number of hours worked, through shorter workweeks and removing children from the workforce, but then goes on to also claim that a slowing of educational attainment is reducing labor quality; things which are in direct contrast to each other. What CATO does get right is the fact that the major solution to improving growth must come from innovation, which they then incorrectly go on to say comes from investments in capital. Capital does not innovate, people innovate, and we will discuss that in much more detail in this chapter and Chap. 9. This flaw in their argument is how they come to the faulty conclusion that even with increases in investments from foreign nations, growth is fated to be perpetually slower than it was. With the entire global economy slowing relative to population growth, such investments will also decrease, so any hope of relying on that as a source of stimulus is just wishful thinking.

On the topic of innovation, refer back to Chap. 6 in the difference between incremental and revolutionary innovations. Since the beginning of the Industrial Revolution, we have really only seen incremental innovations. The advent of computer technology can really be attributed to the use of mechanically automated logic engines first developed by Alan Turing during WWII as a way to decode German encryptions. Even today, at their core, computers still maintain the base functions of a Turing Machine, functional through the use of logical algorithms, but instead of being mechanical, semiconductors are used. Moore's law, developed in the 1960s by Intel co-founder Gordon Moore, states that the number of transistors (a type of semiconductor) which could fit in a single square inch of circuitry would double every 12 months. That rate quickly slowed to every 18 months. Still, while advancements in computer technology have allowed us to improve production and advance human civilization in ways never before imagined, it is still just incremental innovation. Clearly, the shrinking of a computer, or speeding it up, or finding new applications for their use, is just the natural extension of the original Turing Machines. Rather than truly revolutionizing the manner in which people pursue production and consumption in a manner similar to the agricultural or Industrial Revolution, the advancements in computers have merely taken the same economic dynamic created during the Industrial Revolution and applied it to ever-more complex and sophisticated forms of automation. This has allowed humanity to automate not only unskilled labor, but now semi-skilled, and even highly skilled jobs can be done by computers much more quickly than by people. Just as people who worked in textiles changed the nature of their work to learn to use machines for manufacturing, so too is it now the job of the physicist or doctor to learn to use the computers which automate their work—improving the quality and speed with which that work can be done.

This has some flaws, though. As hinted earlier, Moore's law is clearly not limitless. In fact, we are in the midst of reaching the point at which the laws of physics, themselves, are preventing further advancement. In other words, we are approaching the limit of what is physically possible according to the basic physical laws of the universe. The Bekenstein Bound is the mathematical definition of the upper limit of the amount of information or entropy which can be stored in a finite space, down to the quantum level. The speed with which computations can be achieved at this bound, called Bremermann's limit, is the absolute maximum potential of a computer. A 2014 study published in *Nature* by Igor Markov confirms and validates the assertion that we are now approaching these limits.

So, since we have machines which can automate physical and logical processes, it is possible to automate nearly every function humans have in the labor force. The only question is whether or not it is yet cost-effective to do so, and whether the algorithms have been developed to fulfill specific functions yet. As an economic consultant, it is part my job to develop simple algorithms for clients so that they can solve economic problems automatically, which means it is part of my job description to gradually develop my own replacement. This is how many people in the labor market stay relevant, when their more traditional skill sets can be automated more efficiently.

Is it any wonder, then, that labor is less productive? With increased automation, the value and diversity of jobs available has decreased. As noted by CATO, the labor force participation rate has declined in 2008 partly due to changing demographics (aging population), and partly because the jobs which are available simply do not offer what people need in order to survive, so they are choosing to make their own way, but they are doing so without the support structure necessary to be successful at it. A 2017 study from the Brookings Institute has found a correlation between sustained unemployment rates and self-destructive behavior. As detailed in Chaps. 2 and 3, when people have the opportunity to pursue valuable employment, they take it very happily. Long-term inactivity, though, results in poor physical and mental health, and this has contributed to increases in valid disability claims, increased rates of suicide, and increased use of narcotics. This is exacerbated by the "tough on crime" policies implemented in the 1990s which has resulted in exponentially increasing rates of non-violent and drug offenders with a prison record. Since having a prison record makes it extremely difficult to find work (and in many cases legally impossible, depending on a person's field of expertise), this contributes to the continued persistence of labor inactivity.

This is important because they note that lower spending rates have caused what they call a "Keynesian Trap", by which they mean that lower spending means lower hiring, and less demand for workers has decreased the quality of the jobs available, so that people will not take those jobs since they are insufficient for basic survival, and this cycle continues upward. With fewer revenues, investors are simply saving rather than investing, much of their money staying overseas or in tax shelters, but for the first time on record, companies are net savers rather than net investors. As noted by CATO, this is exacerbated by the fact that the price of the maximum capital output potential currently available (i.e., automation) has been decreasing dramatically, which means it takes less investment money to accomplish the same goals, but also that workers are less competitive in terms of creating production.

This, on its own, contributes to an acceleration in the growth of income inequality:

Note from Fig. 8.1, created by the Brookings Institute, that although production levels in manufacturing are increasing, the number of jobs in manufacturing truly are decreasing, especially when compared to the growth in value of the manufacturing sector. In short, the manufacturing sector is growing without the use of people, and that is a trend which is spreading across more sectors than just manufacturing. This has contributed greatly to the decrease in real wages since 2008, which is not without its consequences. As noted in a 2013 study from the BLS, "With the persistent high levels of long-term unemployment, a concern exists that individuals' skills will deteriorate or the individuals will become permanently discouraged from job seeking. High unemployment likely inhibited the usual churn that helps create better matches between worker skills and employer needs, hurting economic efficiency."

The same study states that, "Looking forward to 2022, the U.S. Bureau of Labor Statistics (BLS) expects slower GDP growth to become the 'new normal.' In addition to the recession's impact on potential growth, the labor force participation rate will continue to decline, moderating growth. The need to keep the debt-to-GDP ratio under control will weigh heavily on fiscal decisions. Continued reductions to federal spending will slow growth and cap discretionary spending on projects that could create jobs or research and spawn technological progress. Housing remains one bright

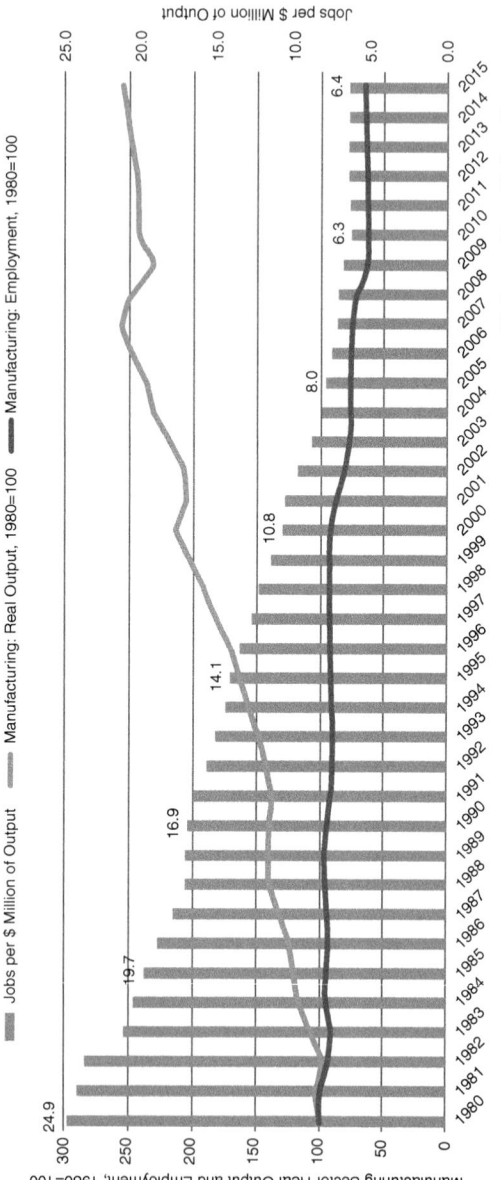

Fig. 8.1 Manufacturing sector inflation-adjusted output and employment, 1980–2015 (Source: Brookings' analysis of Moody's Analytics estimates)

spot in the projections: even at slow rates, population growth implies a need to create homes for additional people, spurring activity in the construction sector." To quickly point out that this statement yet further confirms that we have reached, or are reaching, our maximum production potential under the current economic epoch, and that investments which "spawn techno-logical progress" will be vital to future stimulus, the real point of interest is that last sentence about housing markets being stable as a result of popula-tion growth. The BLS frames this as a positive highlight—the housing markets are experiencing stable growth—great, right? Not so much.

As production rates grow slower relative to population growth, there is a problem. Consider the fact that we already have decreased rates of labor participation (and according to the BLS, that rate is set to drop another 1.4% by 2022 as a result of baby boomers retiring), elevated rates of both unemployment and underemployment, and that production levels are back at normal levels. The implication is simple yet profound: For the first time in all of history we do not need everyone to work in order to meet the demands of the population. Yet, rather than utilize the gains from increased productive efficiency to find new ways to utilize the labor force, we simply let labor assets stagnate; left unused or underused. According to the BLS, "Structural changes occurred in the economy, eliminating many jobs for skilled workers. Technological gains enabled the automation of many jobs, leading to increased productivity and output without generating employ-ment growth. This hollowing-out trend is expected to continue." This has two major impacts on the global economic dynamics of the era: first, that it limits public consumption rates, which are the basis of economic growth; second, and more importantly, that it prevents innovation.

The concern on which people are and will continue to be focused is that of stimulating demand. The population needs to have both the ability and the desire to purchase the goods being produced, otherwise there is no point in producing them—inventories will expand and the companies mak-ing them will stop production until those inventories are sold, if they ever sell, at all. The foundation of the economy is based upon the need for people to pursue the resources for survival, as discussed in Chap. 6, and so every-thing else is built upon that foundation. If people want to buy one good or another, producers will try to find a way to profit from it, and will often go as far as to offer a new type of good, with the risk that people simply will not want it. No matter how much might be invested in new ventures of this sort, it is always demand which defines their success. In fact, when overall demand is lacking, companies will hold onto cash instead of investing in

Annual rate of change

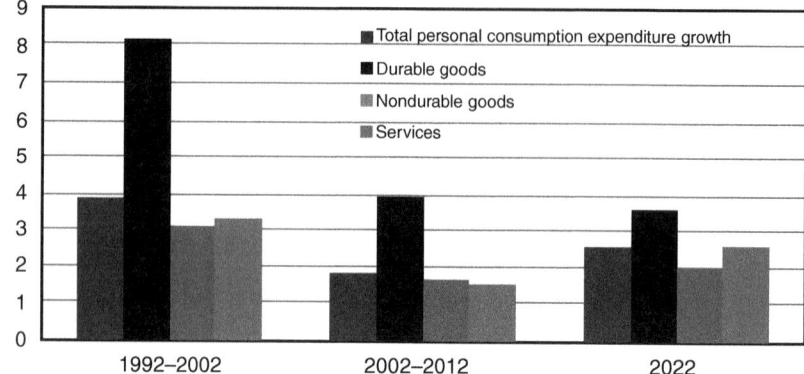

Fig. 8.2 Growth in categories of personal consumption expenditures, 1992–2012 and projected 2022 (Sources: Historical data, U.S. Bureau of Economic Analysis; projected data, U.S. Bureau of Labor Statistics)

any types of new ventures. So, it can be said that demand creates its own supply, but supply will not create its own demand.

With that in mind, by far the largest segment of demand is something called "personal consumption expenditures", which composes roughly 70% of the US GDP. Let me say that again: 70% of the entire US economy is based in personal consumption. So, as we have already stated, demand defines the market, and the market is built on subsistence—the things which keep people alive and healthy. So, this current state in which we are persistently underutilizing labor resources is hurting demand, as shown by the BLS (Fig. 8.2):

Note that personal consumption is divided into three categories: Durable Goods, Non-durable Goods, and Services. Durable goods are those which are intended to last for a while and be used over time. This includes things like vehicles, TVs, furniture, tools, and so forth. This is the category of demand that which slowed most dramatically, because these are the things that people will not need to replace. People do not necessarily need to buy new cars or TVs, often it is simply something that they want, not what they need. So, when people are struggling for money, they will stop buying these things; even when the old ones break, instead of buying a replacement people will get the old ones fixed. If a replacement is truly needed, then they will often buy already-existing ones which are used, and so this does not contribute to demand for new production.

It should come as no surprise that demand for non-durable goods remained the most stable over time, given that this category includes food, hygiene products, and other things which people need to remain alive and healthy. The majority of products that people need, and are will pursue even though it may mean foregoing other things, are in this category. What may come as a surprise is that the largest segment of personal consumption is services, which composes roughly two-third of total personal consumption. Services varied slightly more than non-durable goods, and is actually estimated to increase as a percentage of total demand as the baby boomers age. The reason for this is that services also includes medical care, which is an industry that continues to boom as it garners an ever-growing number of boomers. Like the "good news" about the housing industry which was actually a portent of doom yet to come, the booming medical industry is also a harbinger of things which are less than ideal. Medical care, like non-durable goods, includes things which keep people alive, but unlike non-durable goods, medical care is something which people generally cannot afford on their own. So, as people are living longer, they are consuming greater volumes of medical care that they cannot afford.

So, the government is paying ever-greater amounts through a healthcare system which, by all accounts, could be improved and made more efficient. Combine that with huge "bailout" spending programs that ended up being extremely flawed and wasteful, and the cost of two wars, and tax cuts, all under a single presidency at the turn of the twenty-first century; and the national debt rose to 72.5% of GDP, the highest since WWII, by which time the Great Depression had already ended thanks largely to more effective use of stimulus funding. After the 2008 recession, not so much. Whereas fiscal stimulus would have been expected to help drive up demand and put companies back into production, making them more attractive to investors, as a result of financial mismanagement in the early twenty-first century the government was under much stricter constraints on what it could accomplish. The truth is that the efforts would have been misguided, anyway. Although proper fiscal stimulus would likely have helped lessen the duration and severity of the recession, it would have merely delayed the inevitable. The focus of stimulating production through demand places the emphasis on capital, which helps with growth but does nothing for development or the advancement of the economy toward greater things.

That is where we come to the second item; the more significant and more problematic impact of persistent underutilization of labor resources is a lack of innovation. As the population grows, and production continues to grow though at a relatively slower rate, we will continue to exacerbate many of the major challenges faced by humanity as is advances. Problems in the shortages of food and water, the matter of growing volumes of pollution, the issue of global warming, and so many other challenges we face will not be overcome unless we can allocate resources that stimulate knowledge and innovation toward them, allowing us to develop new solutions. With a stagnant labor force, people do not develop new skills nor do they sustain equal quality of the ones they already had, they will not acquire new knowledge or use that knowledge to provide innovative new ideas. This long-term underutilization of labor resources is set to perpetuate itself and become worse over time, unless we develop new economic infrastructure designed with the intention of fundamentally advancing human civilization into the next economic epoch.

A lot of this chapter has been focused on the United States, but a 2015 study by the Bank of Canada has shown that this trend applies to all of the advanced economies around the world (they define "advanced economies" as including 37 specific nations from around the world). As a global average, the world's advanced economies grew at an average rate of 3.6% per year for decades prior to the 2008 recession. Even after discounting the recession, itself, since 2010 the average global growth has slowed to less than half that rate, growing at an average rate of 1.4% per year. The Bank of Canada cites many of the same reasons for this as other studies, noting that there is actually negative growth in the working-age population among many European and Asian nations, high levels of public debt, technological advances, and low rates of total demand. Like many, they are hesitant to use the term "secular stagnation", and with good reason. The term was first used by Alvin Hansen in 1938 to describe a state of perpetually slow growth, and each time this has been predicted in a post-recession period, it has failed to materialize as a reality. The Bank of Canada, as with others, though, do note that conditions this time are unique, particularly in terms of changing population demographics, differentials in global savings and investment rates, and so forth. The Bank of Canada ends their study by expressing confidence in the ability of monetary policy to stimulate growth, yet this contradicts broader consensus that keeping interest rates low has produced as much stimulus as it is going to, and that any further monetary expansion would simply contribute to the liquidity trap which has been created.

To summarize, the world is in trouble. In a debate hosted by the International Monetary Fund, University of California Berkley economist Brad DeLong states that this is the result of eight things:

1. *Higher income inequality,* which boosts saving too much because the rich cannot think of other things to do with their money;
2. *Technological and demographic stagnation* that lowers the return on investment and pushes desired investment spending down too far;
3. *Nonmarket actors* whose strong demand for safe, liquid assets is driven not by assessments of market risk and return, but by political factors;
4. *A collapse of risk-bearing capacity* as a broken financial sector finds itself overleveraged and failing to mobilize savings, thus driving a large wedge between the returns on risky investments and the returns on safe government debt;
5. *Very low actual and expected inflation,* which means that even a zero safe nominal rate of interest is too high to balance desired investment and planned saving at full employment;
6. *Limited demand for investment goods, coupled with rapid declines in the prices of those goods,* which puts too much downward pressure on the potential profitability of the investment-goods sector;
7. *Market failure in the information economy* – which means markets cannot properly reward those who invest in new technologies, even when the technologies have enormous social returns – which lowers the private rate of return on investment and pushes desired investment spending down too far;
8. *Increasing technology- and rent-seeking-driven obstacles to competition,* which make investment unprofitable for entrants, and market cannibalization possible for incumbents.

As we have discussed and will continue to discuss in this book, however, all these things are symptomatic of a more singular root cause. Simply, we have reached our maximum potential under the current economic epoch and so our growth and development are starting to break down. The systems we have established are becoming irrelevant, and it is now necessary that we replace them. There is a natural next step—something which inherently extends from the current economic epoch that makes the next predictable.

We are starting to see it in the private sector already, but given flaws in the market and the nature of our current system, there must be a concerted national effort to progress. In order for us to take the next step in human advancement, though, we need to reorganize our economic structures in order to make such an advancement viable. As Harvard economist Lawrence Summers states, we need different and unique fiscal policies that emphasize expansionary investments that the private sector simply will not provide. Similarly, the BLS states, "Resurgence in investment will be important to boosting productivity and counteracting the impacts of slow labor force growth and cuts in federal spending." Those investments must be made in people, not capital, and once we look at the cause of our problems deeply enough, the solutions will become obvious, as will the methods by which we will accomplish those solutions.

Bibliography

Baily, M., & Montalbano, N. (2016). *Why is US productivity growth so slow? Possible explanations and policy responses.* Washington, DC: Brookings Institute.

Burke, A. (2017, March 22). *Why are so many American men not working?* Brookings Institution. Retrieved April 08, 2017, from https://www.brookings.edu/blog/brookings-now/2017/03/06/why-are-so-many-american-men-not-working/

DeLong, B. (2017). Sluggish future. *Finance & Development, 54*(1).

Is Slow Growth the New Normal? (2013, October 15). Retrieved April 08, 2017, from https://www.cato.org/events/slow-growth-new-normal

Markov, I. L. (2014). Limits on fundamental limits to computation. *Nature, 512* (7513), 147–154. doi:10.1038/nature13570

Monetary Policy in a Liquidity Trap. (2013, April 11). Retrieved April 08, 2017, from https://krugman.blogs.nytimes.com/2013/04/11/monetary-policy-in-a-liquidity-trap/

Reza, A., & Sarker, S. (2015). Is slower growth the new normal in advanced economies? *Bank of Canada Review.*

Woodward, M. (2013). The U.S. economy to 2022: Settling into a new normal. *Monthly Labor Review.* doi:10.21916/mlr.2013.43

CHAPTER 9

Crux of the Problem

Alright, so we established in Chap. 7 that everyone knows the world is having problems getting their economies to grow and lots of people are looking for a solution. Before we can engineer a proper solution, though, we need to take a closer look at the cause of the problem and understand the nature of growth, otherwise any actions taken will fail to achieve the desired results, potentially even making things worse. This means defining what economic growth is, identifying which part is broken, and studying the implications of what the break is doing to the economy. In order to accomplish this, we will need to look at current models of economic growth.

Macroeconomic growth models can be really intimidating. They are all "mathy", and there are all sorts of variations on each, and complicated criteria that needs to be met, and all of them have valid criticism. It does not make for very good reading, and for the purpose of this book the intimate differences between these models are not relevant, anyway. So instead we are going to jump straight to the relevant parts, which lie at the core of every economic growth model, and the way in which those parts are managed through economic policy. Before that, let us make sure everyone is caught up on the basics, which means defining economic growth.

Growth is a very simple concept: it just means more stuff. If your nation has positive economic growth, it just means that the total value of everything it produces has increased over time. Maybe that means larger volumes of production, or the things being produced are more valuable, but the total value of everything being produced has gone up. Note that this does not necessarily mean anything is better for people, or that you own more stuff, personally, but instead it just means that the nation as a whole has increased the value of its production. For example, let us say you got paid $100 to give 100 chipmunks a hot lather shave in 2016, then in 2017 you were able to shave 200 chipmunks and still got paid $100. The total value of your production increased, so there was economic growth, but your own income did not change. If you got paid more, or if that growth increased the quality of life for the average person, then that would be something else called "development".

So, growth = more stuff; development = better quality of life.

The first challenge is understanding growth, because growth is generally necessary for development to happen. If you want to allocate more stuff to improving quality of life, first you need to make that stuff available, which means you need growth. That is why economic growth models are important: they show us how economic growth happens, allowing us to manage the economy in a manner that produces more stuff, which can then be used to make life better. If managed properly, development should extend naturally from growth, and since that is not currently the case, clearly something has gone awry because merely sustaining a growing population in its current state will at some point become impossible. Even if we ignore the aspect of a continuously growing population that does not overcome the challenges inherent in sustaining that population (like we are currently seeing), economic growth models demonstrate quite clearly that without development, growth will experience "decreasing returns to scale" (which is fancy economics talk that means growth will slow-down unless we do something to improve the tools we are using to stimulate growth).

At the core of every major economic growth model is something called the Cobb-Douglas Production Function (Fig. 9.1):

$$Y = AL^\beta K^\alpha$$

Wherein:

Y = Total production
L = Labor
K = Capital
A = Productivity levels of people using the available capital
β and α = Rates of change in productivity resulting from improved knowledge

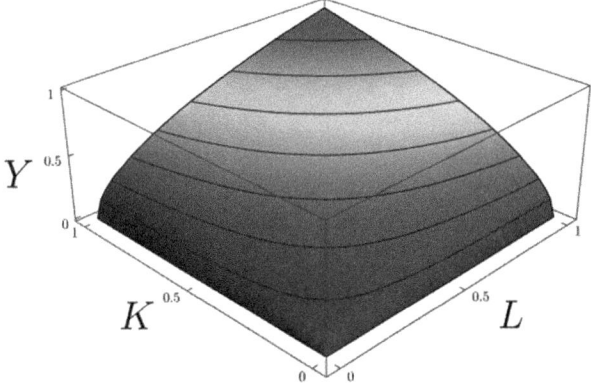

Fig. 9.1   Cobb-Douglas production function

This states that all production is the result of three things: People, Capital, and Knowledge. Some of these terms have equivalents that are used interchangeably; sometimes "people" is referred to as "labor", and "knowledge" and "technology" are both used to refer to the same thing, but capital is usually just called capital. Here is how it works: People produce stuff. It is pretty much a necessity of our continued survival that we need to produce food and shelter and such. That is the "labor" portion of the production function. When people have tools, they are each capable of producing more stuff than they could without them. That is the "capital" portion of the production function. When people learn things, they can make improvements to their tools, which means each person can use things like machinery to produce even more stuff than they could with simple tools. That is the "knowledge" portion of the production function.

This is where things start to break down. Referring to Fig. 9.2, you will note that production increases logarithmically with increasing injections of capital, eventually leading to a point wherein productive output is actually less than the amount of capital input, causing negative growth. This is completely predictable under the law of diminishing marginal returns.

In the grand scheme of things, that is not the important part, though. Sure, it is all very valid theoretical work and has a crucial role as the centerpiece of almost every argument about applied economic policies, but as noted earlier, when you rely on just labor and capital, the whole

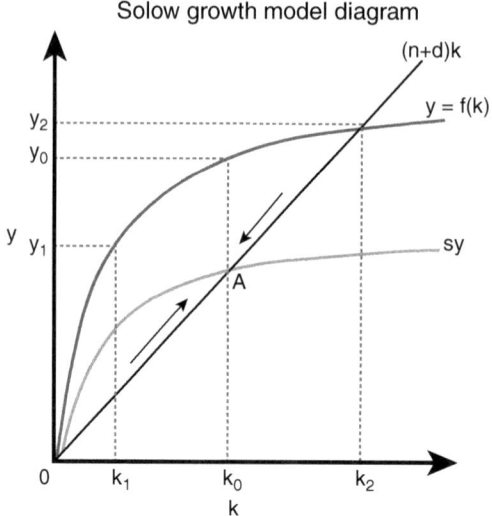

Fig. 9.2   Exogenous growth

thing was doomed from the start. The important part is the relationship between "people" and "knowledge".

Briefly referring back to Chap. 6, how did we stop hunting-gathering and begin developing major civilizations? We learned how to farm, which allowed us to generate more production per person and create gains from trade through the specialization of labor. When we learned to harness electricity and machinery during the Industrial Revolution, the rate of human progress and development exploded because each person produced so much stuff that we could sustain a larger population. This is the key to something called Schumpeterian growth—knowledge is what drives economic growth. This occurs through a process which has been referred to as "creative destruction"—a term coined by Karl Marx—but that term is a misnomer. The simple explanation of creative destruction is that new innovations must inherently replace the currently established structures, thereby "destroying" the old in terms of its value, or even by its physical components, which are then assimilated into the new, more valuable structures. This is not such a revolutionary thing as Marx would have described, however.

Schumpeter describes the process more in terms of evolution than revolution. There is a term called "knowledge spillover" which means that the things you know will be passed on to others by means of working with other people, or teaching/mentoring new workers, and so on. Broadly speaking, it is the distribution of your knowledge to people who already, in fact, have their own unique knowledge set, which not only improves the amount of knowledge that everyone has, but when one person learns new knowledge, they adapt and improve on it by applying it to their own unique knowledge, causing innovation.

Once the population explosion occurred after the Industrial Revolution, we see that the rate of innovation and economic growth also increased dramatically through the digital age. More knowledge means more innovation, resulting in better capital, facilitating the survival of more people, causing more knowledge. Just as with the agricultural revolution, though, the potential advances of the Industrial Revolution (or perhaps, if we incorporate the digital age, we could simply lump it together as the "automation revolution") has reached its full potential, and economic growth is slowing, while population growth increases, resulting in an inevitable equilibrium in which a population is merely being sustained, once again, as discussed in Chap. 7. This equilibrium will not be a pleasant thing to reach, given that the population rate will exceed production, and then the population will have to shrink once again to the point that the production rate can sustain it. A shrinking population, on a global scale, can only result of tragedy—since the resource availability cannot sustain the population, there will be violent conflict to gain control over what resources are available, and mass migrations of people displaced by shortages.

That is the basic idea behind growth, but still does not explain the reason things have broken. To understand why knowledge is not driving economic growth through innovation, we need to look at the current state of economic policies. Managed in terms of fiscal and monetary policy, the focus is nearly entirely on injections of capital focused on "more"—stimulating consumption, production, and employment. This would fall within the realm of something called an exogenous growth model, which are proven to inevitably result in slowed economic growth as a result of diminishing returns to scale. Referring back to Fig. 9.2, we already see that the production increases at a slower rate for every unit of capital input. To illustrate it simply, consider that you have several different options in which you can invest capital. Obviously, you will choose the best one first, and then the next best one, and then the next, and so forth. Eventually the choices remaining are not so good, and you would be better-off just keeping the capital rather than investing it in ventures that will lose money. Currently the primary emphasis of fiscal and monetary policy within the government is precisely that—an attempt to exogenously stimulate growth made ultimately futile by the nature of their approach.

A government can be said to be successful when its people and businesses are successful. When people are earning more money, buying more, investing more, working more, selling more, and so forth—when the economy is growing in a stable manner, a nation's people are benefitting from increased economic activity. Since each economic transaction is taxed at varying rates, we can use tax revenues as a measure of government success. If the government spends money on something and it generates more tax revenues than the amount of money spent, then that was a successful investment because it stimulated economic growth. To get that money, though, the government must institute a tax, which means taking money out of the economy. The amount of economic growth lost as a result of taking money out of the economy is the "cost of capital", because taking money out of the economy means that money is not being used in economic transactions, which will reduce revenues. The term "crowding-out" is used to refer to activities or services fulfilled by the government that would have otherwise been provided by the private sector, but in this case we are talking more broadly. It is not guaranteed, nor is it likely, that the use of financial capital by the government would be the same as the private sector, so the matter becomes very much a concern of where the tax revenues are being sourced from, and what function were they serving. So, under the current system of fiscal policy, the question becomes whether the economic stimulus of government spending exceeds the cost of capital of sourcing those funds through taxation. If tax revenues are increasing, then there has been a positive return on investment. If tax revenues are decreasing, then there has been a negative return on investment. Unfortunately, it is quite clear that governments around the world are generating negative returns. Under the current system, ideally the government would source taxes generating the lowest cost of capital, and then the next highest, and so forth, to ensure that the maximum amount of stimulus is being generated in the private sector; while investing in the best spending options, and then the next best and so forth. Under the current system, ideally this process will continue until return on investment is equal to cost of capital, but even ignoring rampant mismanagement, the approach they use was doomed to fail from the very start.

Monetary policy functions under the same assumptions, working to manage the levels of financial capital available using the same principles of economic growth discussed earlier in this chapter. Functionally, the reality is that monetary policy is also used as a method of making more capital available as a method of economic growth stimulus. The idea is that by buying-up long-term debt issued by lenders, or by decreasing reserve ratios for banks (the amount of money the banks need to keep on-hand), or by decreasing interest rates, it increases the amount of money available to invest. This does not work very well, however, partly due to the Paradox of Credit discussed in Chap. 2 (i.e., higher interest rates creating a self-fulfilling prophecy of higher credit costs from defaulting loans), which extends to a focus on lenders that does little to benefit the borrowers/consumers who stimulate production; and this also extends from the same capital-centric view of growth.

Conspicuously, there is also a distinct failure among many discussing monetary policy to recognize that savings and investments are not the same thing. People concern themselves with the spending compared to saving, just as we have, but then many go on to assume that savings are the same thing as investments. It is said that people save money, it goes into a bank, and then the bank invests it in the form of debt lending, and some even go on to state that people who save money earn interest on their accounts. It is all hogwash stemming from an old model developed by John Hicks called Investment/Savings-Liquidity/Money Preference (IS-LM) in the 1930s, which was intended to illustrate the equilibrium between investing and demand for liquid money. Yes, it is very vague and used mostly as a classroom tool, but the underlying principles still guide monetary policy today. First of all, if bank accounts pay any interest at all, it is in such tiny amounts as to hardly be considered an investment, and often banks will even charge you for your account. Second, savings and investment absolutely must be separated, and treated in a similar manner to the MPS or MPC, for the purpose of economic stimulus. Only a percentage of the money saved is actually invested, and as more of that money is saved rather than invested, the less it is being used to actively contribute to stimulus.

There are bold new methods being proposed, other than the one described in this book, to resolve the matter of slowing economic growth. There are proposals for convoluted and expensive social programs which expand upon the underlying philosophies of The New Deal that established an "economic safety net" and is credited with ending the Great Depression. These are not fundamentally new, however, as they merely make more services available. Clearly this is failing to overcome the problem of advancing growth and development; not only is growth still continuing to slow regardless of the availability of these programs, but the quality of life for people on these programs tends to be below national average. Although these programs do help people during transitionary periods, and help to minimize the severity of problems associated with periods of high unemployment, they create a unique problem in the labor market. They actually contribute to the problems discussed in Chap. 2 through the facilitation of decreased leverage in labor market negotiations. By providing a minimum of certain subsistence dependent on finding gainful employment within a given period of time, people are still forced to find whatever work becomes available just so they can survive once the benefits have been exhausted, but since there are some benefits which are long-term, dependent on maintaining gainful employment employers have been able to offer wages below a living wage. Since government benefits are providing a portion of subsistence goods like food, employers no longer need to pay a living wage, and labor markets are kept out of equilibrium. Some needs are met, but in a manner which does not allow people to the financial freedom to pursue something better via increased labor mobility, investment opportunities, or anything else that would help in the long-run. So, based on current experiences, proposals to expand government economic benefit programs are often rejected.

The proposal that is gaining the most attention and being given the most serious consideration is that of universal basic income (UBI). The idea is simple: Every citizen gets income from the government in an amount necessary to provide the most minimalist of lifestyles. In other words, giving people survival money that is roughly around the minimum cost of living both to guarantee that the economy maintains a minimum stable level of production supported by consumer demand, and to ensure that people are able to support themselves despite increasing rates of automation. In a way, that is how the people of a nation reap the rewards of increased efficiency in production, but UBI does so only by sustaining a base of people able to absorb that production.

Quite bluntly, the idea of a UBI is entirely flawed, but probably not for the reason you think. There are those that will argue that resorting to UBI will cause extensive freeriding, which means people will have no incentive to positively contribute to the economy, instead opting to live exclusively on government funding paid for by those who are active. It is an argument that is used even today to justify reducing or eliminating economic benefits such as food stamps, but the data has shown many times that less than 2% of people participating in these programs are abusing them, and often even less than 1%, depending on the program being studied and who is doing the research. Either way, the ratio is extremely low. The truth is that people want to work, as discussed in Chap. 3; people require a sense of purpose and fulfillment of professional needs to stay sane and healthy, and even if their basic survival needs are financially accounted for, people will still seek gainful employment both to improve their lifestyle beyond the mere minimum required for survival and to provide a sense of purpose in their life. Living in poverty is clearly not a desirable thing, as such miserable circumstances are described in Chap. 2, and so even with a system of basic income, people will continue to find employment, but it is more than that. People need to feel as though they are pursuing a purpose that contributes positively to the continued survival of the human species rather than just the continued survival of their individual selves, as discussed in Chap. 3.

By introducing a constant stream of minimally sufficient income, all it does is facilitate consumption, which is fine for creating stability in a world dominated by automation, but it does nothing for growth or development. The idea of UBI stems from exogenous growth models, stating that by injecting capital into the economy, it will sustain growth. There is a certain degree of truth to this, but also critical flaws. UBI does adhere to the basic mathematics which define the stimulus of monetary velocity by maximizing the multiplier effect of economic policy by emphasizing distribution of capital to those with the highest MPS, as discussed earlier, and during a recession this will help to increase employment. However, there are three major problems. First, and most clearly, it is inefficient. Considering the oft-referenced suggestion by Keynes that during times of slow growth or high unemployment, the government should pay people to dig holes and fill them again, it is true that this would increase consumption thereby stimulating demand for productive labor, but this is a non-value-added stimulus. The digging of holes and filling them again inherently causes a negative return on investment because of this. UBI functions in an identical manner, wherein capital is injected to stimulate consumption without any value-added production. It misses the target entirely on identifying the important components of economics growth, continuing to focus on increasing capital availability, while doing nothing to stimulate knowledge or innovation. This exacerbates the second problem with UBI, in that like all exogenous growth policies, it is subject to decreasing returns to scale, and will very quickly generate negative returns on government expenditures, causing fiscal deficits in the long-run. Referring back to Fig. 9.2, the production growth curve will remain relatively flat, so that any capital inputs exceed production output, resulting in negative returns on government expenditures, making UBI an inherently unsustainable mechanism of economic growth in the long-run. A search through various blogs and newspapers will yield a wide variety of estimates on the nominal costs of UBI, much of it based on completely arbitrary estimates of how much the amount should be and the number of people who would qualify, but they all do one thing in common: they state that existing programs would need to be eliminated. Some state that only social welfare programs like food stamps would need to be eliminated, a more insane estimate states that we would need to eliminate "Social Security, Medicare, Medicaid, food stamps, Supplemental Security Income, housing subsidies, welfare for single women and every other kind of welfare and social-services program, as well as agricultural subsidies and corporate welfare" (essentially all other stimulus spending). Again, although these lack any kind of valid supporting research, every single one of them proposes it as a rearrangement of existing spending. That is not an improvement on anything, as it merely gives the spending a new name. Finally, even capital-based exogenous stimulus policies are beneficial primarily during times of slow economic growth; while during periods in which the economy is already growing quickly, such stimulus tends to contribute more greatly to inflation than to growth, and can overextend growth rates thereby triggering or exacerbating a recessionary cycle. This, of course, results from artificially pushing aggregate demand beyond equilibrium, so that investments in increasing total production capacity increases per unit production costs, and surplus inventories reduce labor demands, when total aggregate consumption fails to remain sustainable at the overextended levels.

The bottom line is that the current approach to stimulating economic growth is approaching, or perhaps has even surpassed, the point wherein managing capital is sufficient to stimulate growth. As a result, a UBI, being merely an extension of the current methods in economic policy, will do nothing to resolve the problems which have resulted from those methods. None of it is congruent with functional economic growth models and, therefore, not congruent with development. In order to fix the problem of slowed growth, and take humanity into the next epoch of economic development, a different tool must be engineered. A whole new approach must be utilized. The economic tool which has been hinted at throughout this book and will be thoroughly detailed in Chap. 10, is a natural extension of the problem as described here, in Chap. 9—a custom solution designed specifically and exclusively for solve the matter of our current approach toward the end of the automation epoch.

To summarize, the problem is that we have reached the maximum of our productive capabilities under the current economic epoch (or are somewhere near that maximum), but we cannot fully shift into the next epoch under the current capital-centric paradigm of growth. The solutions to facilitating the transition into the new era have thus far extended from this same paradigm, which is why they are destined to fail. In order for a solution to work properly it must change the entire emphasis of the economic paradigm and, as a result, the entire functionality of economic policy extending from that paradigm. In failing to do this, our economic production capabilities will fail to sustain the continuously growing human population, and we will fail to resolve the problems that come with that growing population, such as pollution, food and water shortages, and even poverty and conflict driven by overpopulation.

BIBLIOGRAPHY

Aghion, P., Akcigit, U., & Howitt, P. (2013). What do we learn from Schumpeterian growth theory? *Handbook of Economic Growth, 2*, 515–563. doi:10.3386/w18824

Brakman, S., Garretsen, H., & Marrewijk, C. V. (2006). *An introduction to geographical economics: Trade, location and growth*. Cambridge: Cambridge University Press.

Marche, G. (2016). *Introduction to macroeconomics*. Kendall Hunt.

Sahdev, N. (2016). Do knowledge externalities lead to growth in economic complexity? Empirical evidence from Colombia. *Palgrave Communications*. doi:10.1057/palcomms.2016.86

Tanner, M. (2015). *The pros and cons of a guaranteed national income*. Washington, DC: Cato Institute.

Worstall, T. (2016, June 04). *Of course we can afford a universal basic income: Do we want one though?* Retrieved April 08, 2017, from https://www.forbes.com/sites/timworstall/2016/06/04/of-course-we-can-afford-a-universal-basic-income-do-we-want-one-though/#13318969323c

CHAPTER 10

A Prime Opportunity

This is it. This is denouement, the climax, the moment you have been waiting for. Everything so far has led us to this point and now here it is. Not only am I talking about this moment in time as being the most opportune to make the changes necessary, not only am I saying that tangible action must be taken soon lest our continued economic stagnation bring ever-more unnecessary obstacles, but this is the chapter that describes how the whole thing works on a functional level. As noted in Chap. 8, the key lies in Schumpeterian growth, and engineering an economic mechanism which utilizes the vast seas of dormant knowledge to create a perpetual cycle of innovation-based development.

First of all, endogenous growth models state that economic growth primarily occurs not as a result of adding more and more capital, but as a result of improvements in the factors of production. In other words, growth is the inherent result of variation is some growth factor expanding to stimulate increased economic production. Growth creates the resources necessary for development, but through these models, development is what stimulates continued growth. This includes things such as technological innovations—"leapfrogging technologies" such as the availability of mobile phones generating social change in the Middle East, which we now see improving the availability of education, which will be much needed to diversify production in a region whose growth is almost exclusively based on a single depleting resource. As a result, these models do not suffer from the problem of decreasing returns to scale that eventually become

© The Author(s) 2017
M. Taillard, *Aspirational Revolution*,
DOI 10.1007/978-3-319-61771-8_10

self-defeating, since the source of growth is continuously adaptable and not subject to the law of diminishing marginal returns.

Evidence for this exists empirically in comparing national growth and development trends. According to exogenous growth models, poorer countries with lower costs and lower wages, through trade, should attract investments in production or they should have higher rates of exports, resulting in the development of nations to equalize over time. This is not occurring. Quite to the contrary, trendy efforts to stimulate growth in least developed nations (LDNs) by issuing small business loans have actually resulted in debt traps, as the borrowers cannot attract customers for their production because there is not enough growth in the region to absorb the production of the venture. By contrast, the initial development of ancient civilizations came from improvements in technologies, such as agriculture, learning to smelt bronze and then iron, learning to industrialize and program automation, and so on.

Schumpeterian growth is unique in that it specifies improvements in knowledge and the mechanisms by which innovation occur as the primary component of increased production. Whereas other endogenous models may point to any of a variety of possible factors, or perhaps a combination, such as policy structure, or technological breakthroughs, Schumpeterian growth tends to emphasize that these things, themselves, are the result of improvements in knowledge; and that evolutionary learning using the resources available within an economy is at the core.

That is not to say there is not any merit to trade, or even exogenous models. In fact, trade and the investment of capital to stimulate growth are some of the oldest and most fundamentally accepted principles in economics. As described in Chaps. 6 and 8, and hinted at throughout the book, these things do have an important role to play in economic growth, but they have flaws, and present upper limits on the growth potential of a given economic epoch. For long-term growth to occur, endogenous models must be utilized, and as previously stated, we have reached the point wherein not only has capital reached its maximum capacity for growth stimulus, but exogenous models as a whole are now failing to resolve the matter.

To really understand the reason this happens, and the mechanics of how to resolve the issue of managing growth and development, we will need to look more in-depth at some economic models, demonstrating the exact functions of the economy and the flow of production throughout it. Let us start simple, with the basic model of national income flows found in any macroeconomic 101 textbook, shown in Fig. 10.1.

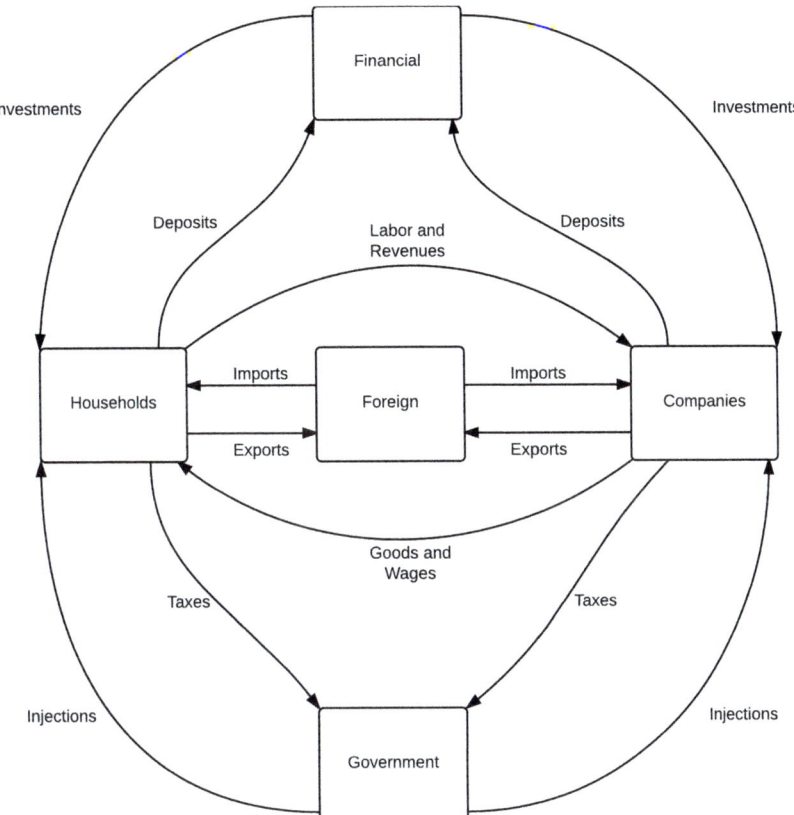

Fig. 10.1 Circular flow of national income

This is known as the circular flow of national income. A nation's economy is an engine of production, and like any engine, it does not matter how big it is unless it is moving. The circular flow of national income is an illustration of how the resources within a nation move between broad economic sectors, so the name clearly comes from the fact that the nation's resources are constantly moving in a big circle. If the flow of resources to or from any sector slows too greatly, or is blocked entirely, then the entire economy seizes to a halt, which is what triggered the Great Depression, the 2008 Financial Crisis, and so forth. It is mostly self-explanatory, so I will give just a very brief summary:

Households Includes consumers and workers. They receive goods and services from companies as consumers, while paying money in exchange. They offer their time and efforts to companies in exchange for wages. They pay taxes to the government and in exchange receive services, and they invest money into the financial sector in exchange for a return on their investments, usually in the form of interest rates.

Companies They provide goods and services to households in exchange for revenues, and they receive labor in exchange for wages. They pay taxes to governments in exchange for services, and investment money in the financial sector in exchange for a return on their investment, usually in the form of interest rates.

Government They receive tax revenues from companies and households, and in return provide services which are generally not provided by the free market.

Financial Includes both depository and brokerage organizations. They receive investments from businesses and households, giving them a return on their investment, usually in the form of interest rates. They then reinvest that money, charging a higher interest rate than they offer, and earning profit on the difference between the two rates (called "the spread").

Foreign Includes the buying and selling of goods from foreign nations. Goods coming into the nation from another nation is called an import, while goods going out of the nation into a nation is called an export, and both are done in exchange for currency. This is functionally no different than any other transaction, except that it occurs between two or more nations.

While the circular flow of national income is undeniably true, it is simplified to the point that it is not very useful for anything other than introducing new students to macroeconomics. So, in order to help explain economic growth, refer to Fig. 10.2, which expands upon the circular flow of national income to illustrate the national income in terms of production growth.

There are a few key points to recognize in Fig. 10.2. First of all, the shaded squares are the elements of the Cobb-Douglas Production Function, which, if you will remember, describes the volume of production

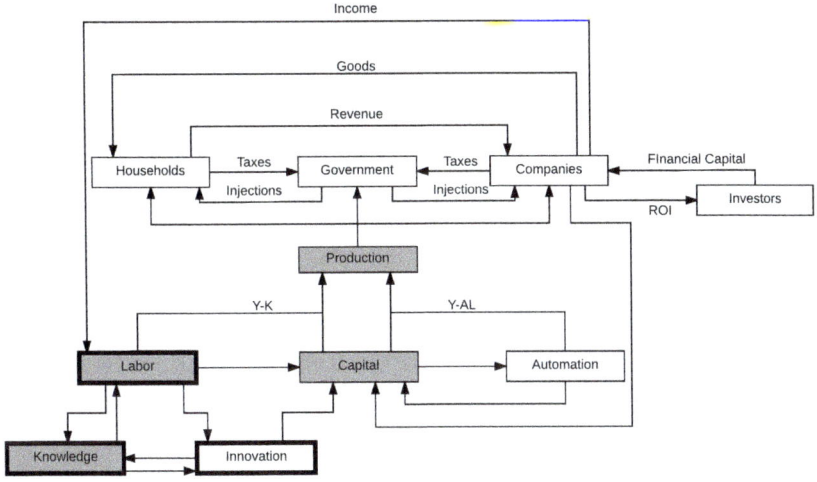

Fig. 10.2 Circular flow of national production

possible and the ratio of labor to capital which contribute to that production. Note that the production function $Y = AL^{\beta}K^{\alpha}$ is split, dividing total production into the ratio of its components. $Y - AL$ is total production contributed purely by capital through automation, while $Y - K$ is total production contributed purely by labor at the labor productivity level available given the available knowledge. The squares in the bottom-left corner with bold borders illustrate Schumpeterian growth stimulus via knowledge spillover.

Over time, ratio increasingly favors capital/automation, as capital-based production becomes more efficient as a result of innovations made through the share knowledge of the labor force. Innovations improve capital, but does not directly improve labor; although innovations help us to improve our knowledge, the innovation itself improves capital, leading to ever-greater reliance on capital instead of labor. Companies invest in capital to become more efficient, reducing total costs, including labor wages, as fewer people are required to produce higher volumes of production, as discussed in Chap. 8, and especially as illustrated in Fig. 8.1.

The top portion of Fig. 10.2 (everything about the production function) is simply the circular flow of capital described in Fig. 10.1, but deconstructed to illustrate differentials in the roles of businesses and households. Specifically, "households" is treated as consumers, while the labor element that is usually included in the circular flow has been singled out as part of the production function. The financial sector in the circular flow model has been divided, to show that it is businesses which are buying capital, and that consumers loans like mortgages are treated as financial products issued by business entities. Investors, by contrast, provide the financial capital to banks and other businesses with the expectation of a return on their investment.

The foreign sector of the circular flow model, with its imports and exports, was left out of Fig. 10.2. Simply, it is not relevant to this chapter, and so including it would only make the graph unnecessarily complex and difficult to read. Quite frankly, whether something is domestic or foreign is irrelevant, since the economic function within the circular flow remains the same.

UBI would alter the current role of government within the circular flow to allocate financial capital to households. As Fig. 10.2 clearly demonstrates, and as was described in Chap. 8, this would merely sustain rates of consumption, perpetuating the continued reliance on capital as the primary source of economic growth. This definitively illustrates that UBI will be self-defeating, as made predictable in the flaws of exogenous growth models when applied to the long run.

As described earlier in this chapter, however, altering the role of government can facilitate the Schumpeterian mechanism in the bottom-left corner of Fig. 10.2 by using the gains from improvements in capital production, triggering a self-perpetuating cycle of innovation, growth, and development. If you want growth, that means facilitating as much knowledge spillover as possible. That means ensuring people are able to acquire knowledge, and facilitate any pursuit to apply that knowledge in new and innovative ways. It means tapping into the innovative potential of the "everyday genius" who has knowledge and aspirations, but not the resources to apply that knowledge and make it available to others. After all, that is the only thing which is still truly unique to us, as humans—innovation. Just about everything else can be automated. That is not a bad thing either, though. By taking all these resources made available through economic growth, and allocating them to people with proposals for such things as inventing, researching, starting small businesses, writing, painting, and so on, we are fully tapping into that mechanism which creates economic growth. On top of that, all these people with ideas, they will all need to hire their own people to help with operations, right? So, now we create a huge volume of small employers, triggering higher demand for labor. This means rock-bottom unemployment rates, and it means more competition for labor, giving workers greater negotiating power in the marketplace, and improving the quality of life for each worker, thus stimulating development. The entire nation then turns into a huge engine driving growth and development, allowing humanity to overcome its most challenging problems.

The only question remaining, and it is a really big question that will take up the remainder of this chapter, is "How does it work?" The basic premise is actually very simple, but there are a lot of details which need to be addressed.

First of all, this all functions as a grant-based program, which will function as a more effective and more efficient fiscal paradigm, able to replace a wide variety of current social welfare program without requiring a UBI. People with an idea of a professional nature who have the aspiration to see their idea come to fruition but without the financial means to pursue it will apply for a government grant. By "professional nature", that means those things people pursue as a career—things which exist within the Schumpeterian mechanism of Fig. 10.2. So, the emphasis is placed on people looking to start a small business or form some other type of new business start-up, people with ideas for inventions or scientific research projects, and cultural pursuits (e.g., writing, painting, composing, etc.) of an experimental nature. In other words, the primary focus is on things which increase free market competition, things which increase technological and scientific advancement, and things which advance the arts.

The actual grant process combines elements of the grant process utilized by the National Institute of Health, and elements of the benefits application process utilized by the Department of Health and Human Resources. A standardized application will be used which people must complete. It is very thorough and includes analysis of at least the following components:

- Detailed description of the project, including details of the specifications and functionality.
- Operational and theoretical feasibility of its success, including financial projections, relevant professional and academic history of the applicant, and grant history.
- Precise budgeting, including required materials, labor requirements, and itemized cost analysis.
- Milestone deadlines, placing dates on the completion of critical parts of the project which can be used to demonstrate timely progress.

- Social and/or economic importance of the project at varying degrees of size and scope.
- Financial need, proving that the cost of the project exceeds the ability of the applicant to fund it using their own income, or traditional loans.

This application process will help to naturally filter out those people who are not legitimate, not seriously dedicated, and/or not capable. The "financial need" portion will also naturally filter out a large bulk of potential applicants, so that the program efficiently stimulates economic growth. That is not to say the program is dedicated entirely to funding small projects in low-income areas either—some entrepreneur might be connecting with ex-NASA engineers for a private space venture. Even though these individuals have disposable income available to them, and qualify for loans of a certain size, a grant would still be needed given the sheer size of the project. There are three broad goals to the application process: First, to provide enough objective information about the project so that the application can be fact-checked for consistency (e.g., if the cost of materials on the application is significantly higher than the market price, then this would be flagged for review of potential fraud). Second, the application is used to force the applicant to demonstrate that they have considered every aspect of the project, can demonstrate its feasibility, and have the ability to manage the project to its completion. Third, the application is used as a method of ensuring the project, itself, has merit that will contribute to growth and development.

For those who complete the application and are not rejected, the applicant will meet in person with a case manager, who will interview the applicant to ensure that they respond in a manner consistent with the application, to help avoid fraud. They will also be asked to either explain or personally demonstrate the feasibility of their project, to help ensure a positive return on government spending by avoiding projects that are highly likely to fail.

After a successful interview, there will be an investigation into the applicant's background: work history, academic credentials, income, monthly bills, credit history, criminal history, and so forth. This functions as one final check to ensure that everything is true and consistent. If the background check is successful, then the project is given the OK for grant funding.

The money itself will be made available via a government-funded debit card which is tied to a system similar to that used in online banking. The card will be prepaid, so that it has a limit, and funds will be released at the milestones listed in the application process, in the amount necessary to get the applicant to the next milestone as described in the budget. Every transaction using the card will be recorded, just like in online banking, wherein the date, dollar amount, and supplier in each transaction is recorded. At each milestone date, there will be an audit of the project to determine whether the project is progressing as quickly as estimated, and to see whether the spending during that milestone period is consistent with the budget. That keeps positive control over the funding, preventing abuse or misuse.

Due diligence is a big deal. There will be certain mandatory milestones at which audits occur, including after initial capital acquisitions, after labor recruitment, after operations have started, and so forth. Once the project is running smoothly for a time, then the audits will largely stop, occurring only at critical milestones in project completion as listed in the application. The final audit will be at the point the applicant can show that the project has provided social/economic benefits roughly equivalent to the cost of the grant. It is at this point a review will be conducted that estimates whether the project benefits will continue to surpass the value of the grant, and the applicant's file closed. From that point onward, it is up to more traditional means to assess the management and performance of the grant-based program as a whole. I suspect informal follow-ups of the program and the applicants will be performed by media, political parties, and so forth, with everyone trying to prove the success or failure of the program.

Any material changes to the deadlines, budgets, or operations will require an application for modification to the original application. This will include a review and investigation process similar to the original, though not as thorough since most of the information has already been evaluated. If, during the course of the project, the applicant discovers that the project is not feasible, or that the budget will unexpectedly exceed the benefits of the project, then funding will be withdrawn.

During audits, if it is discovered that there have been violations in the use of the grant money, deadlines, operations, etc., or should any discrepancies be revealed which materially affect the background check, this will trigger an initial investigation. If appropriate (i.e., there was a violation which resulted as a mistake rather than abuse, such as a missing form), the applicant will be escorted in the filing the modification application, or updating their file.

If it is found that an abuse has taken place, there will be a full and immediate withdrawal of funding, and those funds which have already been spent will be reported to the IRS as a tax debt which must be repaid to the government, with interest. Repayment of these abused funds will be treated in the same manner that the IRS currently manages debts owed. There would also be a criminal investigation for fraud or the use of funds for illegal purposes, and charges would be filed when appropriate. If no criminal activity was found, then no charges will be filed, but the person will not be able to apply for grants again for a period of ten years.

Regarding projects which fail but in which no abuse took place, applicants who have failed in their past projects will require additional scrutiny, but will not immediately be disqualified. The government already funds projects and sometimes they just do not work like one would hope, and it is simply the nature of pursuing a new venture that the possibility exists it will fail. In fact, this is a matter of serious concern among researchers. There is an unofficial mantra among academic researchers that one must "publish or perish", implying that if you do not continuously get research published in journals, then you will not have a career for long. Journals, however, have a strong tendency to only publish research in which the hypotheses are proven correct. Since it is in the nature of research that a person is exploring the unknown in order to answer questions, this problem within the field creates strong incentive for researchers to "fudge" their research in any of a variety of ways to show positive results, or else to only pursue research projects which are already known to have a high likelihood of being true. Ensuring that a failed project does not automatically disqualify a person from future grants will improve the quality of entire career fields by increasing accuracy and increasing willingness to pursue riskier projects. So, if an applicant's project has failed for reasons other than abuse, it will be taken into consideration in future applications, but is not an automatic disqualifier. If projects continue to fail, then that will gradually make it more difficult to be approved for future projects, requiring the applicant to make a much stronger case for the feasibility and economic benefits of their current project.

As for the matter of picking "winners and losers", as hinted at previously in this chapter, there is going to be great concern, and ongoing attempts to corrupt the program for political reasons, partisan or otherwise. That is why the process must be established as a standardized, objective sorting of applicants. As already described, those who cannot so much as describe the intimate details of their project and can demonstrate its feasibility are eliminated from the selection process, as they have failed to prove they know what they are doing and can effectively manage it. Those who have a history of criminal activity (especially crimes of fraud/theft, and people with felonies in the past ten years) will find it difficult or impossible to be approved in order to prevent abuse. People who have an extensive history of failed projects will find it increasingly difficult to be approved, in order to prevent waste. People who have the ability to finance their project using traditional means will be disqualified, since funding such products would produce no actual added value that would otherwise not be generated, yet would require the use of spending tax funds, thereby generating negative growth for the nation—higher taxes and higher government spending with no added economic value is generally accepted to be a bad thing. The most difficult, and perhaps most subjective, portion of the application process is demonstrating the social benefits of the project. Describing the economic benefits of a project is simple, such as estimating the number of jobs that will be created, the wages of these jobs, financial projections, etc. These are things which an applicant should have no trouble, if they are truly qualified to manage the project to its completion. Describing social benefits is more difficult, and may pose a challenge especially for those pursuing grants in the arts. Inventors and researchers can easily refer to the ways in which their work will contribute to a population's health, education, or other measure of qualify of life. The arts is a little tougher, though. There are many studies showing that expanding the arts in a nation or a region shows a demonstrable impact on improved economies, higher test scores in schools, improved community health, and so forth. Research by the Arts Council in England demonstrated that 78% of kids who participated in a music program improved their scores in core Science, Technology, Engineering, and Maths (STEM) subjects, that participation in arts programs improved the symptoms of specific medical conditions like dementia and Parkinson's, and that the arts industry in the United Kingdom produced roughly GBP12.4 billion in economic stimulus. These studies are always done in terms of "the arts" as a whole (i.e., painting, writing, composing, sculpting, etc.), rather than attempting to present the value of a single art project. There is also undeniably an inherent importance of specific artists who contributed greatly to their field, for example Van Gough and his contributions to painting. Not everyone is willing to quit their job to live in desperate poverty in the pursuit of their art like Vincent van Gogh, but how would Van Gogh be able to communicate the importance of his work if a grant became available to provide him with painting supplies and a basic wage? Admittedly, my solution to this is not perfect, but in objectively assessing the value of funding a specific artistic project, there are two broad assessments which suffice well enough. First, that the artist has had some minimum degree of success and recognition, but not so much that they are able to fully dedicate themselves to a project without devastating financial hardship. Second, the artist must be able to demonstrate that the project they are pursuing offers something new to their field—that it is unique in some way, contributing new methods, techniques, styles, or other trait which has not been used before; conclusively generating new knowledge through which innovation might occur.

Artist Stuart Semple agrees that this is a challenging issue to properly incorporate the arts into such a grant model in a manner which protects against fraud, but which then does not put limits on the value of the arts. Since art represents life and society, he feels that forcing artists to incorporate themselves into society and find ways to fund their own art is critical to the contributions that art makes. By funding artists, the implication is that the artist is being put into a situation of creating art and removed from that which should inspire their art. Yet, he also acknowledges the importance of the Arts Council, which helps sponsor artists. Those artists are not subject to a bureaucratic application process, though, which Semple feels would also take some of the "life" out of the arts. So, it seems as though the previously stated approach to addressing the arts is the best currently available, though improvements are likely to present themselves.

Grants are already issued by government agencies, but only for things needed by the government. There is little or no stimulus that results from this because the areas of knowledge being funded are very narrow, and only for very specific purposes, using a tiny percentage of the available knowledge pool. Assuming the knowledge created is not classified and kept from the public, it still does little or nothing to stimulate broader innovation. It is for this reason that some people are skeptical about their efficacy, and choose instead to opt for a subsidy-based model, in which expenditures on certain qualifying projects are instead funded through a tax subsidy (people claim the costs on their tax forms and get compensated). The first, and most obvious problem with this, is that if people could afford the cost of their project in the first place, they would not need the grant. Remember that the entire point is to tap into the collective pool of knowledge currently unutilized, which includes a vast number of people without the financial means to get started. The percentage of Americans who live paycheck-to-paycheck ranges somewhere between 66% and 75%, depending on which study being cited. These individuals live without any ability to allocate funding to projects even in the short-term, much less have the ability to quit their jobs to pursue such a project in the first place. So, in one way, the subsidy method is more selective in that it is available only to those who already have the means to fund their projects. In another way, however, the subsidy model is less selective in that it provides no mechanism to ensure the validity or feasibility of a project, becoming easily abused. The grant-based model, when more generally applied as a method to stimulate economic growth instead of merely as a medium of government contracting, actually decreases the need for many subsidies, thereby decreasing government spending and improving free market functionality, which will be discussed in this chapter.

To wrap up this chapter, let us look at crowdfunding. Crowdfunding is a new medium of fundraising in which a person puts their fundraising purpose on a website, and the general public makes donations in varying sizes. Not only is crowdfunding a bottom-up form of funding, making it a great contrast to illustrate the importance of implementing a grant-based model, but it is actually a great way to illustrate the current shift in cultural and economic dynamics in the global society—helping to show that people are already primed and ready for this kind of a transition. Besides crowdsourcing for personal matters or charities, we are also seeing an increase in capital investing using the bottom-up online style of fundraising medium, connecting venture capitalists and angel investors with entrepreneurs; and we are seeing more researchers use it to fund research projects. The problem with it from a logistical point is that crowdsourcing is extremely subject to the ebb and tide of internet society—tending to be swayed more toward such things as Exploding Kittens (a card game by The Oatmeal), while everything else flies under the radar. You will get the occasional project which goes viral, but the crowdsourcing sites will even tell you that you should rely first, and foremost, on your personal network of people. This structure—the Avon Products model of business—is not a great choice for an economic structure. There is also very little necessary to post a project to crowdsourcing sites. You do not have to show estimated budgeting, specifications, justifications, timelines, or anything. Including some of these things can be helpful in allowing you to raise funds, but one does not have to demonstrate the potential impact. As a primary economic structure, this would give a lot of room for abuse. So, although these privately operated mediums of funding research, businesses, and so forth are increasing in popularity, they have critical flaws which prevent them from becoming a primary source of economic growth. They demonstrate perfectly that there is a need for a new medium of stimulating innovation and knowledge, and that the public is seeking new and creative ways to facilitate advancements in human potential, but do not function in a manner which makes such advancements possible on a large scale. In order to accomplish this, a top-down model is required, as described in this chapter.

BIBLIOGRAPHY

Bop Consulting. (2016). *Measuring the economic benefits of arts and culture: Practical guidance on research methodologies for arts and cultural organisations.* London: Arts Council.

Howell, S. T. (2017). Financing innovation: Evidence from R&D grants. *American Economic Review, 107*(4), 1136–1164. doi:10.1257/aer.20150808

Marche, G. (2016). *Introduction to macroeconomics.* Kendall Hunt.

Monetary Policy in a Liquidity Trap. (2013, April 11). Retrieved April 08, 2017, from https://krugman.blogs.nytimes.com/2013/04/11/monetary-policy-in-a-liquidity-trap/

Ranganathan, J. (2013, August 06). *Crowd-funding for research dollars: A cure for science's ills?* Retrieved April 08, 2017, from https://blogs.scientificamerican.com/guest-blog/crowdfunding-for-research-dollars-a-cure-for-sciences-ills/

Sahdev, N. (2016). Do knowledge externalities lead to growth in economic complexity? Empirical evidence from Colombia. *Palgrave Communications.* doi:10.1057/palcomms.2016.86

CHAPTER 11

Future Potential

Before a non-fiction book like this gets approved, a proposal is written and the publisher sends that proposal to other experts in the field. That means several economists assigned by Palgrave Macmillan reviewed a summary of the contents of this book before the project was approved for contract. These reviewers remain anonymous for the sake of avoiding conflict and drama, so I am afraid I cannot give proper credit where it is due, but the most critical reviewer of this project (who was called Reviewer 1 by the editors at Palgrave) was the only one to state that the project should not be approved. I state this not in resentment, but because the final conclusion of Reviewer 1 does much to emphasize the importance of what Reviewer 1 says. The reason Reviewer 1 gave for stating the book should not be approved was a lack of clarity in the proposal. Even as Reviewer 1 was concluding that the book should not be accepted, though, regarding the content itself, Reviewer 1 says, "It is true that knowledge is the main source of economic growth. Numerous studies in the field of economic growth and development attest to this fact: A casual search in Econlit or any other economic database will spit out hundreds of journal articles on the topic. See also Ashraf, M. (2014) Formal and Informal Social Safety Nets: Growth and Development in the Modern Economy, Chapter 3 for a literature review and citations."

The point is that even the critics of my work agree with my underlying proposal for the need for a new economic structure, and they even agree with the structure I am proposing. Still, as noted in the very beginning of this book, so too shall we note at the end that this book will cause

© The Author(s) 2017
M. Taillard, *Aspirational Revolution*,
DOI 10.1007/978-3-319-61771-8_11

controversy. The debates will exist primarily on topics of the exact results which will occur after the change is implemented. Reviewer 1's primary concerns existed in the fact that I did not elaborate well-enough on the outcome of the change, and how they will compare to the current structure. Reviewer 1 wanted to know more, and had many questions regarding the fiscal implications of altering our approach to growth and development stimulus. My response was, "Spoilers! You will have to buy the book to find out!"

Now wonder no longer, for I shall behold the future by divining the runes! In other words, let us use some funny-looking economic modeling to determine how the proposed change to the current structure will influence a variety of issues related to the future the national economy, starting with the impact inferred from a combination of both exogenous and endogenous growth models.

The honest truth is that we are talking about a paradigm shift as significant as the agricultural or Industrial Revolution—an advancement in our approach to human growth and development—that it barely resembles anything we have known in the past. No one cannot predict the exact innovations which will occur as a result of this change during the coming epoch, but I can tell you the methods by which they will occur, and what those methods will mean for the national economy.

With impeccable timing in 2017, just as Palgrave Macmillan was finishing editing the original manuscript of this book, a study by Sabrina Howell entitled *Financing Innovation: Evidence from R&D Grants* was published in the American Economic Review which strongly supports the importance of using a grant-based model in stimulating global growth and development. In this study she references prior works which note that early-start-up firms are statistically more likely to spur lasting innovations, yet they also suffer most greatly from financial difficulty during the research and development phases of their formation. As these firms are first forming, private capital investors see them as having comparatively long development cycles, a longer than average time to break-even on the initial investment, discouraging private investment in such firms. Her own research expands upon this by demonstrating that government grants of early-start-up firms. Howell demonstrates that small early-stage grants allows firms to "invest in reducing uncertainty", meaning that the financial risk associated with entrepreneurial efforts is reduced. Her data definitively demonstrates that these grants "have large, positive effects on cite-weighted patents, finance, revenue, survival, and successful exit". In other words, grant recipients tend to have a higher rate of becoming healthy, self-perpetuating firms over the long run; it only takes a bit of assistance getting over that initial financial risk.

Howell's research also demonstrated that the reduced risk of grant recipients tended to attract private capital investors in greater volume, facilitating a faster and more innovative expansion phase for these firms. Her findings show that grant recipients were roughly 100% more likely to attract subsequent private capital funding than their non-recipient counterparts, and that greater degrees of pre-grant financial constraints were strongly correlated with a larger relative increase in future operating revenues and patent filings. The macroeconomic implication is that the grant-based model proposed in this book will create greater incentive from the private sector to once again become net investors rather than net savers, improving the health and sustainability of the free market capital investment sector.

First of all, there will be a lot more free market competition. The economy as a whole will become more efficient, more productive, and more innovative as potential entrepreneurs enter the market. Not only will this put greater emphasis on small businesses with higher growth potential than already-large corporations, but it will force all companies within the market to learn to more effectively adapt to changes in the market, causing the market itself to improve in its functions. Besides innovation through competition, there will be a vast increase in the volume and variety of something called "disruptive technologies". The word "disruptive" here does not mean that it will cause bad things to happen, just that the technologies being developed will replace previously common technologies, resulting in a disruption of the market for those technologies. For example, the invention of the printing press was a disruptive technology that revolutionized the world by making books widely available and largely eliminating the need for scribes. At any rate, the increased volume and diversity of inventions and research will directly generate new knowledge. In addition to further improving free market competition by making new products and operational functions available, this will have a direct impact on the national quality of life. New inventions and new knowledge that help us to solve challenges and improve upon existing methods will allow us to not only live longer, healthier, and hopefully happier lives; also made possible with increased levels of production which means more resources will be made available to allocate to such things as education, healthcare, infrastructure, and other things which improve a nation.

All this will, of course, have an impact on the amount of productivity per person, the efficiency with which we use our national resources, and also the cost to producers (which then translates to an impact on the prices to consumers). The increased competition, improvements in methods, and improved technologies will create increases in average production per capita in the same manner as the agricultural or Industrial Revolution, but this will occur at a much more rapid pace. Improved efficiency means more production output per unit of resource inputs, which means lower costs to producers, which means lower prices to consumers; all the while the market evolves to provide ever-improving products.

With each new major breakthrough, production potential will grow and, with it, development will improve, as well. It is in the nature of the proposed structure that these breakthroughs are a natural outcome to be achieved regularly simply by emphasizing growth through innovation rather than through capital gains. Given that the proposed structure creates a cycle of continuously-increasing knowledge, the rate at which advances occur within the nation will accelerate over time, allowing us to overcome the most pressing threats to human existence. No longer is our greatest concern as a species beating other animals to sources of food and shelter, but rather we look to global cataclysms such as global warming, meteor crashes, massive volcanoes, and so forth. Even the inescapable matter of continuous population growth which will need to be addressed in the distant future has the potential to be overcome, but we must have the economic structure in place so that people might be able to achieve these goals.

We talked about economic gravity in general terms in Chap. 6, but when we use those principles within the context of the economic structure being proposed within this book, the results are profound. Historically, capital tends to concentrate in very singular ways, so that opportunities to fund innovation are held in the hands of a select few who have resources, for those reasons described throughout the entirety of this book. The "financial need" clause of the grant application process (necessary for reasons of ensuring economic advancement through endogenous stimulus rather than the perpetuation of capital-based exogenous growth, as described in Chap. 9) changes that dynamic, however—making investment resources available to those who can effectively utilize them, but without interfering in the typical dynamic of free market capital allocations. In other words, as already stated, this new structure will have the greatest impact on those who do not have the resources to pursue their project. By nature of the law of the diminishing marginal returns, and the economic dynamics resulting from differentials in the MPC, it also means that those who earn the lowest incomes, or who live in the lowest-income areas, will have the most significant economic impact. This is entirely due to the principles of economic gravity.

Let us put this in simpler terms. Considering the processes of economic gravity described in Chap. 6, it stands to reason that a successful venture will attract both capital and people. It is also a well-founded, if not obvious, fact that creating ten jobs in an area with very high unemployment will have a greater positive impact than creating ten jobs in an area with very low employment. Creating ten jobs in an area of high employment, even assuming you can find people in the area to fill those jobs, would create far less stimulus as a ratio of the existing volume of economic production than creating ten jobs in an area of low employment. As a result, the clause of financial need in the application process has uniquely important results. First, it helps to stimulate employment in areas of high unemployment, reducing the need for social benefits programs. The increased economic activity in blighted areas will attract the resources and tax-generating economic activity necessary to help revitalize these regions which, by itself, has been shown to reduce problems such as crime rates, thereby improving quality of life by means other than economics.

It is important to note that we are not talking about a "redistribution of wealth" here. None of this is referring to "taking from the rich and giving to the poor". What this structure does is reallocate tax funding already in use to stimulate economic growth through innovation. The method by which this is most effective is merely a ratio scale based on financial need for assistance to pursue innovative ventures. So, instead of nomadic pockets of wealth that continuously accumulate, there is constant wealth being developed through free market forces, as the free market is intended to function.

Economic gravity will also help to stimulate impoverished areas by the methods this already naturally occurs in a limited manner. With a greater volume of people pursuing independent ventures seek locations for their operations, a sizeable percentage of them will look to low-cost areas (though I will not say most, because another sizeable percentage will look to areas where they know people, they know the market, and have access to a labor pool with the right skill set). This movement of capital to low-income areas will function as a seed which will grow to attract additional capital and labor. The greater volume and geographic locations of this stimulus will result in a more even distribution of growth and development, helping to reduce the number and severity of those pockets of poverty which exist, both in urban and in rural areas.

Given the greater ratio of improved economic stimulus in impoverished areas which will result, this naturally translates into a greater ratio of improved tax revenues. The job opportunities made available will require a workforce with the basic skills to perform those tasks, and since many of these areas struggle with funding their schools already, the increased funding for school resources, and the improved job opportunities providing incentive to kids to finish school will improve education, particularly in those areas which need it most. The importance of education has been reiterated so many times throughout history and around the world that it has become something of a chanted mantra. Yes, education is important. In fact, since "education" is the word we use to describe the process through which information is passed from one person to another, it is one of the primary components of economic growth through innovation—it is a core element of the Schumpeterian mechanism described in Chap. 10. There are two major problems with education as we think of it today, however, at least in terms of its role as a mechanism of economic growth. First, that people tend to think that formal schooling is the only viable source of information through which one might become educated; and second, that the acquisition of information is the only mechanism through which growth and development through innovation occurs. In other words, we are not only ignoring the majority of our primary economic growth mechanism, but we are ignoring the majority of the only part of that mechanism which actually gets attention.

First, people tend to think of formal schools and universities as the sole source of education. It is a common misconception that more schooling increases something economists call "labor quality". The idea is that the data shows that more educated people earn more money, so they must be more productive, meaning that they are higher quality labor. While it is true that formal schooling is a great way to obtain diverse sets of new knowledge contributing to our ability to innovate, particularly through high school and the first two years of university, everything past that point tends to be a different type of schooling. Once a person has determined the field in which they will specialize, the knowledge they receive at school also tends to be specialized. The longer you go to school, the more specialized you become, until you complete your PhD, at which point you have demonstrated that you are a preeminent expert on one particular topic within your field of expertise. That is not so different from obtaining specialized knowledge by other means such as apprenticeships, trade schools, and so forth. If it is a person's career field to function as an electrician, and they go to trade school for a few years to achieve that, it does not mean they are less productive than someone who went to university for 12+ years to get a PhD, it just means that the person with the PhD pursued a field that requires a greater degree of specialized training before they can be fully functional in their field. Still, this misconception on schooling and education contributed to a huge increases in the volume of people attending university, which then flooded many fields of expertise which the medium of university education could provide.

It does not matter why it happened or who is at fault, but all this has contributed to a huge percentage of those born between 1980 and 1995 incurring unreasonable amounts of student debt and becoming disenchanted not only with the value of post-secondary education, but also with the plutocratic tendencies of the global governmental structure. As briefly discussed in Chap. 9, knowledge spillover occurs in many more ways, however. The most common method of knowledge transfer—and the one which was being referred to when the term "knowledge spillover" was dubbed—was simple observation. By simply observing others doing their work, a person is able to acquire information about the cause and effect of the manner in which the work is being done. This is the basis for many traditional types of education, such as apprenticeships and internships, which have become underappreciated in many developed nations. There are also hybrid models which combine apprentice-based and university-based sources of education, called trade schools. Even for those who are not beginners, observing those who are experimenting in their field of expertise, or who do things a bit differently, or even those who work in different fields all provide sources of information which are incorporated into an individual's own set of knowledge which can then be applied in innovative ways. So, labor creates information, and information contributes to improvements in labor; but information also contributes to things which are brand new—innovation.

Although the spread of knowledge is largely ignored, or at least misunderstood as a contributor to economic growth, it does have the formal schooling system to provide at least one type of education that is broadly respected, and the other forms of education do still exist, though any nation would be better-off by providing more emphasis and respect to a variety of diverse mediums of education from a cultural perspective. This is a matter which will largely resolve itself, however, as the changes proposed will stimulate the cycle of endogenous Schumpeterian growth, giving greater incentive to acquire information from a variety of sources as a greater variety of opportunities become available. This happens as we focus on the creation of new knowledge through innovation. As described in Chap. 9, the emphasis of this new economic structure is on facilitating innovation by helping people afford their pursuit of invention, research, entrepreneurship, and the arts. In order for people to innovate in these areas, though, they first need to have a base understanding of what they are doing. In most cases, the inspiration for ideas that people have will result from the skills they have already acquired and the things they have already learned, as described through the process of knowledge spillover. However, it is likely that even experienced individuals will need to learn some new skills they have never used before, or hire someone who has those skills. A computer programmer with an idea for an invention might be able to program the algorithm that makes the invention function, but would likely need to hire someone who knows how to put the physical objects together, or contract with someone who knows how to operate and maintain the machinery that manufactures custom-built molds or tools. With vast new volumes of innovation being pursued, there will be much greater need for skilled labor in order to provide the unique resources needed to create these innovative new things. This will naturally create a shift in the labor market to improve diversification in the types of jobs that are in demand, which inherently requires greater diversification in the types of education being pursued. So, even though the old adage states that education stimulates innovation, Chap. 9 demonstrates that education is stimulated by innovation—not only by driving demand for education, but the very nature of innovation itself provides new information from which others can learn. That is how the cycle works: creating opportunities for innovation creates new knowledge others can use to produce additional innovation which creates additional opportunities and so forth. People who have an idea for an invention, a research project, a new business, a piece of art or literature, would be able to provide a detailed proposal and completed application to receive grant funding, including the cost of living, and then provide regular progress updates in order to renew their grant. Such a dynamic would effectively turn our entire nation into an engine for innovation, new technologies, intense free market competition, and artistic genius. Clearly a majority of people are not so inclined, but by distributing the sources of economic growth across so many people, each will need their own microeconomic infrastructure to facilitate their own operations—in other words, demand for employment will skyrocket as so many people essentially become their own firm. This is the model of the twenty-first century, and we are already in it. The tech sector is already ahead of the game, with pioneers taking early steps toward this economic model—Elon Musk, Bill Gates, Mark Zuckerberg, and others have all taken it upon themselves to be the drivers toward creating a nation built on dreams. Companies like Google, Microsoft, and Apple already operate their companies in this exact same manner. A 2017 study on the economy of Colombia from the Harvard Center for International Development tested and proved that expanding the rate of knowledge spillover increases the complexity of an economy, so that there is greater diversity of industry and increased competitiveness in global trade for a wider variety of industries by driving peoples' ability to expand and improve operations. The study illustrates this as a solution for the "Dutch Disease", which is a state in which a nation has a huge advantage in a single industry, or a very narrow set of industries, so that the strength of those exports shifts the value of currencies in a way that makes that nation's other industries weaker in global trade. As described throughout this book, lower diversity of jobs, and lower demand for employment from a diversity of industries, has been a drag on economic growth. Facilitating knowledge spillover and innovation is the solution to resolving this problem. This is the new era of human advancement.

Finally we come to the big question on the minds of economists and policy-makers: What are the fiscal implications? How much will this cost, will it cost more than the current system, what will be the implications on social safety net programs, etc. It is a valid question, but it is also a big question that does not have a single "soundbite"-type answer. First, recall from previous chapters that we are concerned with return on investment—increases in tax revenues that exceed the amount of money the government spent. Since government spending is done using tax dollars, we want to see as little spending as possible, but we also want to see the spending that is done generate the greatest amount of economic activity possible (i.e., hiring, working, investing, consuming, etc.), all of which generate tax revenues. Even if the government is using debt, so long as they generate more value than the interest costs on that debt, then it is a good thing. So, throw out the whole argument of "more spending vs. less spending"; because we are not worried about spending—we are worried about finding good investments, and a good investment is one that grows in value beyond its original cost.

The proposed structure will cause some immediate improvements in spending quality, but the real impact will be gradual. In the long-run we will see a decrease in total government spending, but a sharp increase in the value of the spending being done. In the more immediate future, there will be subtle changes that result in dramatic improvements to the nation's economy. As noted regarding the logistics of the proposed structure, and the manner in which growth will be distributed discussed earlier in this chapter, two things will occur. First, there will be opportunities to cut spending on inefficient social support programs. Although they are important under the current structure, they will become largely unneeded and irrelevant under the new structure. This reduction in spending would roughly offset the first one to three years in which the projects being funded are working to generate positive returns, which will then contribute to the positive gains on government spending.

The short-run impact will also include a more typical exogenously-based stimulus. As described earlier in this chapter, the distribution of grants to people with financial need to pursue projects will result in increased spending and investing from people who tend to have a higher MPC. The increased spending stimulus will have the same impact as the types of fiscal stimulus attempted under today's structure: since these individuals spend a higher percentage of their total available money, the amount of economic growth is compounded via the multiplier effect. In other words, each dollar is being used in a greater number of transactions, causing the amount of economic stimulus to multiply beyond the amount originally spent. The rate at which each dollar is used in more and more transactions is called monetary velocity. So, if you take the total supply of money and multiply that by its velocity, the total economic value will be equivalent to the size of the economy—the GDP. So, by the very nature of the proposed structure, we would see an immediate increase in economic stimulus via an increase in monetary velocity by way of the multiplier effect.

There is something fundamentally different, though, about this immediate effect. The difference is that the money being spent is not being spent on consumption. A majority of it is being spent on investment capital intended to generate greater value over time, or to directly create value-generating jobs. This is particularly important because it represents a total departure from fundamentals of current economic dynamics in that this approach to increasing investing does not require an associated increase in savings rates, as would normally be predicted by the IS-LM models. So, whereas only a percentage of total savings are allocated to investment under the current economic structure, it is required that 100% of the capital being made available is invested in economy-stimulating activities, as assured by the funding distribution method and periodic audits described in Chap. 9.

The short-term spending will still occur, given that any new venture has start-up costs, but the spending will be of higher quality—creating additional value over a longer period of time. The ways in which the spending is done will also change, not only being allocated to basic consumer goods that sustain consumption, but also directed to sectors that produce business materials, propping-up domestic manufacturing, since these people requiring specialized or custom materials will likely not have import/export savvy, leaving them incapable or unwilling to find foreign suppliers, at least in the short-run.

Over the course of this new economic epoch, for decades or possibly centuries to come, the increased speed with which innovations are developed will contribute to much greater efficiency in operations and resolve many problems that currently exist today. Gradually, government spending will decrease by a significant percentage as it incorporates these improvements or is replaced by privately developed solutions (as opposed to the current process of privatization which tends to be code for "some elected official found a way to profit from tax-funded government operations"). For example, innovations in the way we approach healthcare and military operations (two of our largest national costs) will not only allow for more effective ways to meet goals, but to do so at lower costs, thereby resulting in lower total government spending in areas not directly related with economic stimulus programs. These trends will eventually, little by little, improve government efficiency and cost reduction efforts, permeating every operation thereby facilitating efforts to reduce the total size of government. In other words, although a smaller government is not necessarily a better government, a better government will result in a smaller government. On top of that, as these new innovations increase productivity per capita, the volume of economic activity will increase, allowing for either higher tax revenues without altering tax rates, or equivalent tax revenues while lowering tax rates. Either way, there will be a reduction in the reliance on debt spending, reducing the volume of interest costs associated with government debt, and potentially even the ability to eliminate government debt entirely in the distant future.

The entire history of human existence has brought us to this point. We have advanced our knowledge and developed innovations which makes our lives better through increased production potential. We have invented new forms of capital that are more efficient at accomplishing tasks than people, but in the process we seem to have forgotten the critical role that people played in making that happen. We have lost our way, now almost entirely focusing on advancing our capital, but without the knowledge and innovation that people bring this is a futile effort, and we are now starting to see the result of this failure. By better understanding economic growth, and the role that people have within it, we can turn the nation into an engine of self-perpetuating innovation, rather than continuing to struggle to maintain production growth sufficient to sustain a population which is doomed anyway, lest we focus our efforts on those unique human traits which have allowed us to adapt and survive from the start.

Investing in capital builds only wealth. Investing in people builds empires.

BIBLIOGRAPHY

Howell, S. T. (2017). Financing innovation: Evidence from R&D grants. *American Economic Review, 107*(4), 1136–1164. doi:10.1257/aer.20150808

Sahdev, N. (2016). Do knowledge externalities lead to growth in economic complexity? Empirical evidence from Colombia. *Palgrave Communications.* doi:10.1057/palcomms.2016.86

Conclusion

So, that is everything. Hopefully it makes sense now why multiple approaches had to be used to explain this in full. There are aspects of the application of economic principles which just make a lot more sense when you first understand what drives them, but at the same time, if you look just at the individual motivations then the economic functions (or dysfunctions, as the case may be) which naturally direct us to the conclusions which were drawn could never be made. It is only by considering both, and their interactions together, through which a full and proper grasp of this proposed change to the foundations of our economic structure can be formed. The first half of the book provided both descriptions and detailed examples of how people function in the current economic structures, and the way that this would change under the structures proposed in this book. The second half detailed the econometrics, specifically explaining how and why the current structures are really starting to crumble, and then provides the logistics of how a solution can be implemented.

Hopefully now it also makes sense as to why I encouraged you so strongly to share this book with someone who otherwise would not have been likely to buy it themselves. It is by expanding the scope and diversity of the knowledge in people that they are able to incorporate new information into the context of their pre-existing set of knowledge, allowing them to interpret and apply the new information in unique ways only made possible by them, that new innovations will be possible. It is this process of innovation which is key—the spark of idea which a person will sometimes have, and when they have a true skill and passion for that idea, then it becomes

© The Author(s) 2017
M. Taillard, *Aspirational Revolution*,
DOI 10.1007/978-3-319-61771-8_12

something greater, it becomes purpose. It is only when people aspire to realize their purpose—when they work to see new visions become reality—that human civilizations will advance. This is the one thing that makes humans truly unique from other creatures, and from our own creations: our ability to understand abstract principles and apply them in new ways without ever having to directly observe it. So it is this which must be at the core of our future.

The data demonstrates quite conclusively that we have reached the end of an era, and that this is causing our current systems to cease to function properly. New systems which facilitate the pursuit of innovations and purpose by providing people with resources are necessary to move into the new era. Simply making resources generally available at all times and to all people just in case they have an idea, though, is functionally no different than a broad fiscal stimulus package aimed at increasing consumption. To function properly, such a system must be dedicated to those who already have a specific purpose in mind, which inherently takes the form of a grant-based system of facilitating the pursuit of purpose. It is to ensure that people have the freedom they need to make their visions become a reality, and the end result will permeate every aspect of human life. It will fundamentally change the way in which humanity, as a whole, pursues subsistence.

When we learned to farm, we gradually phased-out hunting-gathering, but that was still very common all the way up until mass production became possible and it was applied to the agricultural industry. Thus automation took over and hunting-gathering became almost exclusively something done for enjoyment than out of necessity. Farming was still relied upon heavily, but much of it was automated. The more we advance, the less we rely on those things which were once at the center of the human experience. Rather than hunting and gathering, we would farm and grow our own food, allowing civilizations to form, but then we took the next step and subsistence meant specializing in just one aspect of that civilization and trading your own skills for the other things you need. Now that our needs are met, and increasingly they are becoming fully automated, people are staying relevant by becoming innovative and coming up with their own ideas to develop new technologies to replace the old. Our specializations—the careers we choose—are shifting from traditional forms of labor toward the operating of machinery which performs that labor, and now much of the development and operation of machinery is automated by computers, so that in the current era our jobs have become an ongoing effort to create our own replacements in the workforce.

This means gains in production that are not being utilized, and labor resources which are being underutilized. By applying the former to the latter in the proper way, we create something entirely new. The human experience becomes focused around the pursuit of new and advanced ideas. Just as farming did not fully eliminate hunting, and automation did not fully eliminate farming, nor will this change fully eliminate automation or traditional forms of work. In the early stages, it will simply be an increase in the number of people pursuing their aspirations and bringing new progress, which will actually increase demand for the volume and diversity of workers, thereby improving labor markets in the exact manner predicted by Adam Smith in 1776—by increasing competition for labor among employers. This will increase the value of jobs by increasing wages, benefits, and working conditions through the free market; giving greater incentive not only for people to actively join the labor force, but to pursue training and education so that they might better fulfill the roles required of them. Then, in the later stages, as more people learn more skills, we will continuously find ways to improve upon new technologies, and more people will be inspired to develop their own ideas. So, increasingly we will automate greater volumes of functions, and a greater percentage of people will dedicate themselves to improving upon the human experience. This is what is necessary for humanity to overcome its most pressing challenges—those things which we must eventually face that pose a mortal threat to our very existence.

All of this is achieved only by first facilitating the pursuit of purpose. That means helping would-be entrepreneurs to create start-ups; new-entrants to the market which will increase free market competition and continue to force existing companies to evolve and improve through the process of creative destruction. That means helping would-be inventors and researchers utilize their ingenuity and knowledge to create things which are entirely new, expanding the bounds of what is possible. That means helping would-be artists and musicians and writers to communicate back to us expressions of who we are and generate new insights into what we might become. It is by investing in people who aspire to do more that these things can be achieved.

I will conclude this book with one final profile of a real person, this time in its raw form, rather than as a narrative. Through the ages of human civilization, we have forgotten the names of so many who have contributed to our advancement, but we remember forever those about whom books were written. So through these pages let the ideas and experiences of these people become ever immortalized, so that their ideas might continue to inspire as many people as possible, and contribute to the knowledge available to current and future generations.

Thank you again for reading.

Profile: Glenn James

1. Why did you originally get involved in accounting and what was your career path up until the point you decided to go independent?

I got involved in accounting like most people, accidentally. I thought I wanted to be an engineer, but I didn't really know why, it just sounded smart to the 18-year-old me. Once I started taking a few courses, I decided it wasn't really for me. At that point I had to rethink everything. Some friends suggested getting a business degree. Healthcare didn't interest me, so it was business sort of by default. I took a couple of accounting courses and for some reason the concepts made sense to me.

While still in college I had the epiphany that I should work over the summer in a job related to accounting. My father suggested I reach out to a placement agent/recruiter with accountemps. I went to their office for a skill set screening test and within a couple of weeks was placed on a long-term assignment taking over as an accounting clerk for the summer while someone was on maternity leave. The following summer, I was placed on an assignment at an automotive Original Equipment Manufacturer (OEM) as a corporate receivables clerk. The following summer I was offered an accounting internship with that OEM. During that internship, I worked on a project with team members from a Big 4 accounting firm, who offered me a job to join their audit and advisory services practice shortly before I graduated with my accounting degree. I worked a little over two years as an associate and was promoted to senior associate. Shortly before the end of my third year, I was recruited to join another Big 4 accounting firm as a senior associate in their internal audit advisory practice. I spent over 11 years at this firm. I became a certified internal auditor while I was a senior associate and was promoted to Manager at the end of my third year. I was a manager for about two and a half years before I was promoted to Director. I spent the next five plus years as a Director. My next step was Managing Director and I started progressing through the internal interview process, when I decided to head in another direction.

2. Why did you decide to go independent? What were the factors you took into consideration, and how did the benefits appear to outweigh the risks/costs?

I decided to go independent because in progressing to the next stage in my career at the Big 4 accounting firm, it was becoming more and more necessary to spend less time helping clients execute projects. I wanted more balance, but with the metric structure in place to measure performance of high performing Directors and Managing Directors, New Business Development is valued much higher than knowledge and project excellence. Projects cannot go poorly, but that responsibility is pushed to managers. I wanted to go independent so I could balance business development and client support without regard for someone else's metrics and requirements in measuring success. I wanted the freedom to take projects because they are interesting, not just based on how many staff people could be assigned, average rate per hour, gross and net margin, etc.

The freedom to choose outweighed the certainty of the paycheck. The certainty is only an illusion anyways. I had plenty of colleagues over the years who were strong performers one day and less than year later, were being "counseled out" of the firm for not meeting enough of their targets.

3. Do you find that being independent gives you greater freedom in your career, does the change in your professional role create more restrictions for you, or is there some trade-off?

Flexibility and freedom are synonymous being an independent consultant, but there is also stress. It's not all rainbows and unicorns. The success is all mine, but so is the strain, challenges, and worry. I like the ability to choose projects based on interest, not just profitability (which the big firms will say they do too, but try to get approval for a marginally profitable project that isn't with a "strategic priority" account. Good luck.). This freedom has allowed me to grow more as a better consultant too. Being at a Big 4 firm, you are shoehorned into a service line and expected as a Director or MD, to serve and sell projects within that service line. The service line is your sponsor in the firm, your reason for having a position. The leaders of service lines are not charged with growing the firm. Of course they are indirectly and say that is their first priority, but they are measured and compensated first and foremost on their performance as service line leaders. So if an accounting advisory (AA) partner has to choose between placing their best resources in an AA project and helping a fellow partner to staff a project they need help with, the AA partner will always choose their own project first, even if the other project is a better fit for the staff or the firm.

4. As an independent, have you hired staff or contracted some functions? How does this compare to the number and types of staff you utilized while working with a major firm?

I contracted some administrative functions (website development, legal counsel, etc.). For now, we are keeping the firm to myself and my partner. We are planning for growth, but in the short-term will contract out for temporary or project-based consultants as the need arises. Compared with the Big 4 firm, I used resources from several different disciplines. A Big 4 firm provides access to individuals with broad and special skill sets. Staff resource needs vary greatly project to project. The one thing that was pretty consistent though is that Big 4 staff are hard charging, very smart, motivated professionals. There are very few there that are just living in a job year after year like you may find in industry.

5. Has your business/clientele grown more rapidly as an independent than it was while working at a firm? Has the type of clients/target market changed in any way?

Growth is difficult to compare to a Big 4 accounting firm because of the sheer magnitude of their size. On a personal level, my client revenue is comparable to my managed revenue while I was with the firm. The types and targets are the same, but the marketing of services is different. I am able to offer direct engagement delivery by the most experienced resources. The Big 4 firms operate as a pyramid delivery model by design. Their revenue, organizational, and compensation hierarchies demand this type of model. This means the least experienced resources deliver the greatest number of hours, while the most experienced (Partners and Directors) generally spent very little time in delivery of any engagement. The model on most consulting/advisory projects is approx. 2% partner time, 3–5% Director time, 5–10% Manager time and the remaining time split between Seniors and Associates. So approx. 80–85% of the project hours are provided by resources with less than five years of work experience.

I am able to flip that model upside down.

6. What is the ultimate goal you have for your current professional direction? How does this differ from working with a firm?

The goal of working at a Big 4 firm is to make partner. You spend your whole time until you make partner, striving for it. It is touted as the pinnacle of a Big 4 career. Now I am a partner in my firm and it does feel great. But my goals now are to grow my business, my way. Not significantly different goals; increase revenue, create meaningful opportunities, help clients solve complex issues. What is different however is how to accomplish the goals.

7. Is there anything else you'd like to say? In particular, do you have any observations regarding the degree of professional freedom you have now compared to while you were working at a large firm?

On a personal level, I have much more flexibility. Compared to other jobs, professional consulting at a Big 4 accounting firm offers incredible benefits; high salary, opportunity for advancement, wonderful benefits, and personal flexibility. There were some chances to work from home and as you progress higher in the firm you gain even more flexibility over your schedule. However, there was also a tremendous amount of time spent on admin (timesheets, expense reports, performance management, incessant internal meetings) and long hours into the evening and weekends working on proposals. The initiatives and more accurately, fending off the initiatives is one of the biggest time wasters. I spend all of my time now on value added activities to my business. I don't attend meetings or fill out customer relationship mgmt. Forms online just because some partner wants to justify spending millions on a tracking system. I now spend my time developing relationships, which is funny because that was the intention of the Customer Relationship Management (CRM) system the firm used, but it was such an admin burden, teams spent half of their development time recording "activities" and half of their time actually developing.

People sometimes ask me if I work more now. The answer honestly is no. I spend my time much more strategically. It's for the benefit of the business or it doesn't happen.

AFTERWORD

As already discussed in this book, and already well established as a proven fact, when looking at the development of per capita production potential over the ages, there have always been absolute limits. As previously stated in Chaps. 6, 7, 8 and 9 (and vaguely supported by the productivity equation described in Chap. 3), given the knowledge and capital of any given era, there is a maximum amount of anything which a person can produce. During the agricultural era, each person could only tend to so many acres of crops in the time available to them. Even with the help of domesticated horses or oxen, and using tools of wood and metal, there was still a maximum limit to what could be produced by each person—a maximum average production volume. These upper limits are nothing new or groundbreaking; they are essentially required reading as an economics undergrad.

It is also not a new thing to consider the absolute lower limits of production possible, though it is more depressing. The lower limit is defined by the minimum volume of production required to sustain a living population. Any production level below that point will cause a total collapse in any population for a period of time until production levels can be increased, if that even becomes possible. The minimum levels of production were far more relevant centuries ago when people were concerned about their population surviving the winter, or the drought season. During those eras prior to the Industrial Revolution, when we had maxed out our per capita production potential, the maximum limit was not so much more than the minimum limit, and any disruption of nature, or even reckless land usage resulting in poor farming conditions, would be disastrous.

© The Author(s) 2017
M. Taillard, *Aspirational Revolution*,
DOI 10.1007/978-3-319-61771-8

For some reason this lower limit is not discussed as frequently as the upper limit, nor is it discussed as much as it used to be long ago. Perhaps it says something about our perceptions of bountiful production in an era of prosperity. Perhaps it is simply that people focus more on pushing the boundaries of growth rather than preventing potential shrinkage. Perhaps the implications of what would happen should production fail to continue to support the current size of the population is simply too depressing. Regardless of the reason that the lower limit has not been subject to the same theoretical research as the upper production limit, it holds important insights.

I promise we will get to the interesting stuff in a bit, but first we need to talk about taking these absolute upper and lower limits of production to the national or otherwise aggregate level. On the high end, yes, there is the ubiquitous LRAS curve which models the upper limit of production potential given any changes in the market, as previously discussed in Chap. 6. The lower limit of national production is the smallest amount of production possible necessary to sustain a population. If your population is decreasing as a result of shortages of food or water or whatever else, then your nation has dropped below the minimum absolute production limit. The population must inherently shrink to the point that it can be sustained by the available resources. This is something often seen in ghost towns; villages that were built on once-productive mines, railways, or lakes. Once the source of production was used up or replaced in some way, the people were forced to leave, though typically there is a small number of people who remain that can subsist on what little remains. Sure, these towns were never fully self-sustaining, but no economic entity is—trade is a critical aspect of even the national economy. So remember: If production increases, the population increases, as we have seen throughout the entirety of this book; but if production decreases, then so must the population. Even if there are not enough resources to sustain a population, though, in economics they will not necessarily consider this a shortage.

What exactly is a shortage, then? Looking through all the introductory texts, it can be seen that professors are teaching people that a shortage occurs when price is lower than equilibrium (Fig. A.1).

In other words, if the price level of some goods is set at a level wherein more people want to buy it than companies can produce, then that is the definition of a shortage. By our current definition of a shortage, price just needs to increase to equilibrium level, and the shortage is gone, regardless of whether the needs of the people are being met. This is what students are

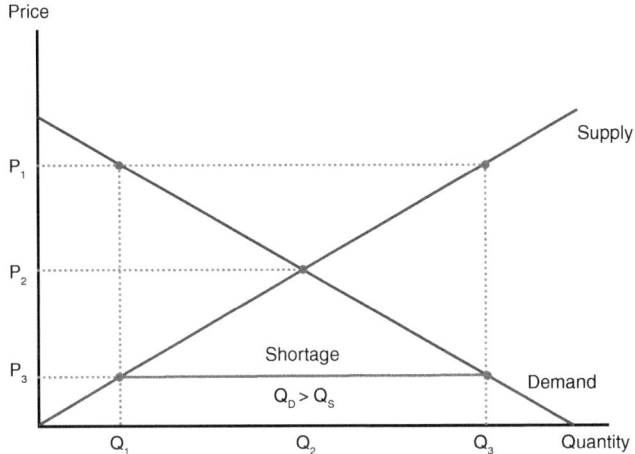

Fig. A.1   Introduction to shortages

being taught—this is what is being published in college Intro to Econ textbooks. This definition of a shortage is preposterous on its surface, and history is ripe with examples of peoples living (or not) during times of famine who would disagree. For example, in 2011 roughly 260,000 people died of starvation in Somalia as a result of famine, and in March 2017 at least 110 more have died of food shortages. Yet, according to the textbook economic definition of a shortage, so long as the price of food increases to the point that only those who have access to food can afford it, then the equilibrium has been attained and the shortage no longer exists. To this I say Poppycock!

If the price of food increases beyond the level that people cannot afford it, then there is a shortage. If, for example, there is a drought, and the supply of food decreases to the point that the equilibrium price is above that which can be afforded by the general population, then that is a shortage. Even though prices may be at equilibrium—even if the volume of production and the volume of consumption are balanced at a given price level—the current state of things is simply that total production levels have dropped below an aggregate absolute minimum. I will say that again: Even if price and supply of food are in economic equilibrium, if total production drops below the absolute minimum national demand, then there is a shortage. In such a situation, regardless of supply and price, there are people in demand of food who will be denied, and this will cause a nation to fail to sustain its population. That is a shortage, regardless of what your Econ101 textbook has to say about the matter. The population of the nation will shrink to that which can be sustained by the available supply, causing a drop in total national production potential as a result of a shrinking labor force. This, then reduces production volume even further, with far-reaching implications. It cannot be denied that this absolute lower limit exists, and thus we have established that the current definition of a shortage is insufficient, and that there is a lower absolute limit of supply to which it becomes possible to refer in order to redefine shortages.

By contrast, the absolute upper limit on supply would be any volume of production so high that the nation simply cannot use or export any additional volume. This is clearly inefficient and all production exceeding that point would have to be scrapped, or dumped, or otherwise wasted. It is a rare time in history that such a thing is possible, but many developed nations do live in such a time, such as seen when goods are produced, then the price is reduced again and again yet there simply is not enough demand, even giving it away for free. Thus, there is an upper absolute limit of supply at which point any additional production will go to waste. This occurs most commonly in agricultural markets, since producers must sell their goods before they spoil; and particularly before the commodities futures markets were established, a lot of food would go to waste because producers would grow more of a particular item than consumers wanted at any price level before that food went to rot. By contrast, exceeding the upper absolute limit on production of something like clothing allows producers to store the surplus and reduce production levels until the surplus sells, or else if storage costs or costs associated with stopping production at any time are too high, the clothes can be donated. Still, it is theoretically possible that a clothing manufacturer produces so many that even charities are overburdened and refuse to accept any more. It seems extreme, but then it was not so long ago that the idea of having too much food available seemed like an extreme concept. That absolute upper limit on production does exist, even if we are not currently at risk of surpassing it.

Let us look at this from the perspective of demand. We are going to stick to the examples of food, because there are real historical examples of food shortages, and I do not want to get too abstract yet. So, for any individual, the minimum absolute limit on demand for food is that which is necessary to keep them alive. They will demand that much at any price, and if they cannot afford it then they will probably steal it, since survival instinct is a pretty strong motivator. Starvation drives people to do desperate things, even resorting to cannibalism. By contrast, the upper limit for the demand of food is the point where the person has gorged themselves and physically cannot eat any more, even if they want to. It is a bit grotesque to think about, but we are talking about the extreme limits, so it is unavoidable, but if a person simply eats so much at every meal that they will become physically ill given another bite, then that is their absolute upper limit of what they can possibly demand, and anything more will resort in food waste as well as harm to the individual.

Moving to the macro level, we can see that the outcome of these absolute limits of demand are the same as the absolute limits of supply. If total demand for food drops below the absolute minimum necessary to sustain a population, then it means you are losing some of your population. If the absolute upper limit of total demand for food exceeds what the population can possibly consume, then it means much of that food is going to waste.

Figure A.2 is a little graph I made to illustrate the point, using the example of a food shortage.

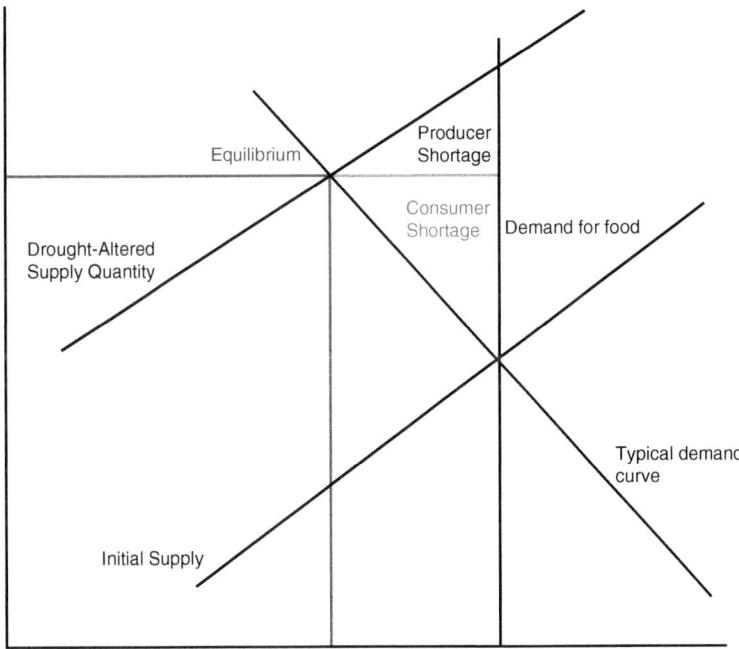

Fig. A.2   Absolute shortages

Note that the minimum demand for food is perfectly inelastic, and that there is a spread between the demand for food and the equilibrium. Since equilibrium price is normally lower at minimum demand, and price increased as a result of decreased supply, there is a shortage of food even though price and supply is at equilibrium. This naturally leads to a couple more unfamiliar concepts: Producer Shortage and Consumer Shortage. This actually works in a similar fashion to producer and consumer surplus, but in reverse. The producer shortage is the loss of value that they should have earned if the demand for food was being met at the altered supply curve. The consumer shortage is the amount of value lost by paying too high a price for food if supply were at equilibrium with absolute demand.

When the lower absolute limit is exceeded, that is where government aid usually comes into play. Government agencies will buy supplies, thereby providing additional funds to producers, while consumers get supplies for free or at a reduced price, thereby reducing the consumer shortage. When the upper absolute limit is exceeded, mechanisms are put into place to help absorb the surplus. Arguably the futures market on commodities was developed in part to mitigate the losses that were being experienced each year, though government intervention in the form of buying surplus production has also been used in the past with questionable efficacy.

Accepting the idea of absolute limits on supply and demand for things like food and water is the easy part. These things are essential to life, meaning their demand is perfectly inelastic to price. It does not hurt that there are real, historical examples of these things occurring, either, giving these concepts an applied importance. If we accept that, though, then what about other things which naturally have higher price elasticity? For example, is there an absolute limit on PlayStation 4 game systems? Is there a point at which demand for the PS4 will not increase no matter how low price goes? Believe it or not there is actually precedence for this. Due to urban legends surrounding a devastatingly bad game (E. T. for the Atari), and the attempts to determine whether the legend was true, it became common knowledge that game producers dump surplus games and game systems that they could not get people to buy even at deep discounts. No matter how low prices go on things like entertainment, there is still a limit to the amount that the population can or will possibly consume.

Could there possibly be a lower limit, though? Could there be a volume of video game systems so low that people will be willing to spend any price for it? As far as I can figure, the answer is no, but there is something which applies that gives a similar result. When video games come out with a limited edition version of some game, people place collector's value on it, just as they do with collector cars, cards, etc. In 2016, Martin Shkreli paid $2 million for a music album by the Wu-Tang Clan. Why so much? Because it was the only copy ever created with legal protections against reproduction. In another example, the Lamborghini Veneno is not the fastest or most powerful car ever created (although it does rank among the top), but it is by far one of the most expensive cars ever produced. With only 6 ever made, they retailed at over $3.5 million each. Exceeding that price range requires a person to search for vehicles with historical or collector's value; in 2016 the record sale price for a car at auction was $35.7 million for a 1957 Ferrari 335S—a racing car of which only 4 were made, and this one in particular had history in the record books. Although such rarity of luxury goods does not create the desperation in which people would be willing to pay literally any price, it does create an extreme lower limit of volume at which price increases exponentially, despite failing to achieve a true absolute.

It is easy to see validity of applying absolute limits to food, clothing, heart surgery, and other things which are naturally very price inelastic. When it comes to comfort and novelty goods, though, while there is an upper absolute limit, there does not appear to be a lower absolute limit. As expected, low supply results in high prices, but there does not appear to be a point at which reducing supply would cause consequences to the population. As explained, there is something vaguely similar, in which price increases quite dramatically, but whether or not there is any true equivalence is yet uncertain. Perhaps supply for that Wu-Tang album did drop below an absolute minimum, at which point people resorted to the digital equivalent of stealing—pirating illegal copies. Perhaps severe differences in wealth create a comparative absolute lower limit, in which the luxuries of a few draw the ire of the majority of people living just above the absolute lower limit of things like food, until a correction is made. In any of these cases, though, there does not appear to be a fully equivalent absolutely lower limit of supply for comfort goods which will limit a nation's ability to sustain its population.

So what does any of this have to do with this book? Everything, actually. As we have already discussed, per capita production levels really only experience fundamental increases with the introduction of some new type of technology: agricultural, industrial, and digital epochs. We have also discussed the fact that we are able to meet the needs of the population without everyone working, creating a challenging situation with unemployment. Using the new economic dynamic discussed in this book, we will see increased production from both capital and people, and it will grow at an increasing rate. We have surpassed the minimum absolute limit long, long ago; but with this new approach it is likely we will start to push the limits of the upper absolute limits. Fast changes in technologies, invention, research, and investing will be a major driver of improved sources of economic growth, and will cause new economic epochs to be surpassed in shorter periods. It is quite possible that under the paradigm proposed in this book, advances will be made which allow all needs to be met to their fullest, bringing us to the absolute upper limits of production on all things, taking us to the next economic epoch.

Granted, at this point we are talking about the kind of long-term planning more attributed to futurists than economists, but the logic is sound. In a world where all your needs are met to their fullest no matter how low the price, including resources for pursuits such as research, entrepreneurship, and artistic ventures … well, it will be an immensely interesting time for economists because by today's standards such a scenario would be considered peculiar, indeed. In the meantime, though, as we close this book, let us remember where we are today, and emphasize the need to first tap into the innovation of the public so we can take our very first steps in an era of advancement that will drive us to meet those long-term goals.

BIBLIOGRAPHY

Alamogordo, T. D. (n.d.). *New Mexico city finds buried treasure of Atari games.* Retrieved April 08, 2017, from http://money.cnn.com/2015/09/01/technology/atari-et/

Leonard, D., & Hordern, A. (2015, December 08). *Pharma's bad boy exec paid $2 million for Wu-Tang Clan's new record.* Retrieved April 08, 2017, from https://www.bloomberg.com/features/2015-martin-shkreli-wu-tang-clan-album/

Marche, G. (2016). *Introduction to microeconomics.* Kendall Hunt.

Press, A. G. (2017, March 05). *Somalia: 110 dead from hunger in past 48 hours of drought.* Retrieved April 08, 2017, from https://www.usatoday.com/story/news/world/2017/03/04/somalia-110-dead-hunger-past-48-hours-drought/98739642/

Seal, A., & Bailey, R. (2013). The 2011 Famine in Somalia: Lessons learnt from a failed response? *Conflict and Health, 7*(1), 22. doi:10.1186/1752–1505–7-22

INDEX

© The Author(s) 2017
M. Taillard, *Aspirational Revolution*,
DOI 10.1007/978-3-319-61771-8